February Making Books with Pockets

The series of monthly activity books you've been waiting for!

Enliven every month of the year with fun, exciting learning projects that students can proudly present in a unique book format.

Each month has lessons for art, writing, reading, math, science, social studies, and poetry.

Contents

Michelle Barnett, Caitlin Rabanera, and **Ann Switzer** have taught first, second, and third grade. Their teaching experiences have involved working with limited-English-speaking students from many parts of the world, supervising student teachers, and conducting inservice sessions for colleagues. They are currently teaching in Southern California.

EMC 585

Evan-Moor® EDUCATIONAL PUBLISHERS

Helping Children Learn since 1979

Authors: Michelle Barnett, Caitlin Rabanera, Ann Switzer
Editors: Marilyn Evans, Jill Norris
Copy Editor: Cathy Harber
Illustrator: Jo Larsen
Designer: Cheryl Puckett
Desktop: Shannon Frederickson

Congratulations on your purchase of some of the finest teaching materials in the world.

For information about other Evan-Moor products, call 1-800-777-4362 or FAX 1-800-777-4332.
Visit our Web site www.evan-moor.com for additional product information.

Here are ideas for celebrating some of the special days in February.

February 2 ______ Groundhog Day

Read a book about Groundhog's Day. Check in the newspaper to see if the "official" groundhog in Punxsutawney, Pennsylvania, saw its shadow. Take your students outside and see if they can find their shadows. Will winter continue longer?

February 7 ______ Laura Ingalls Wilder's Birthday

Begin reading *Little House in the Big Woods* (first book in her series). Talk about life during the time in which Laura Ingalls Wilder lived. How was it different? How have things changed?

February 17 ______ Random Acts of Kindness Day

Talk about what this means and what we might do to observe this day. Encourage children to report kindnesses done to them.

February 20 ______ First American to Orbit the Earth

On this date in 1962, John Glenn orbited the Earth three times. In 1998 he became the oldest person in space when he flew on the shuttle Discovery. Bring in freeze-dried ice cream to share with your class. Talk about what it's like in outer space.

February 29 ______ Leap Day

As a class math challenge, imagine that a person was born on February 29 and could only celebrate birthdays on leap year. The person has celebrated six birthdays. When was he or she born?

Black History Month

February is Black History Month. Read the book *Teammates* by Peter Golenbock.

National Snack Food Month

Make a chart of healthy snacks. Make a healthy snack in class each week.

February

Sunday	Monday	Tuesday	Wednesday	Thursday	Friday	Saturday

How to Make Pocket Books

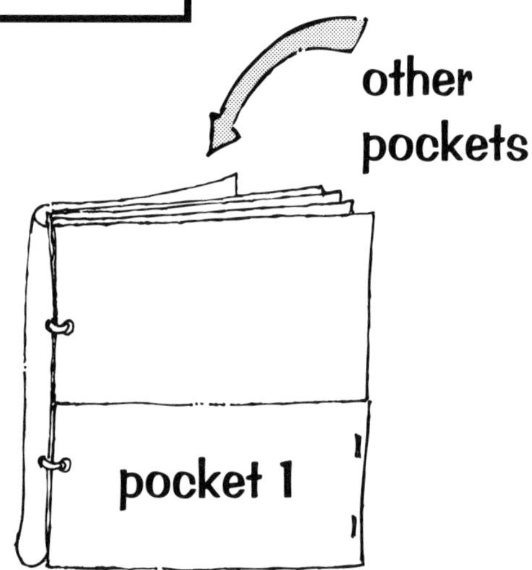

Each pocket book has a cover and three or more pockets. Choose construction paper colors that are appropriate to the theme of the book. Using several colors in a book creates an effective presentation.

Materials

- 12" x 18" (30.5 x 45.5 cm) piece of construction paper for each pocket
- cover as described for each book
- hole punch
- stapler
- string, ribbon, twine, raffia, etc., for ties

Steps to Follow

1. Fold the construction paper to create a pocket. After folding, the paper should measure 12" (30.5 cm) square.
2. Staple the right side of each pocket closed.
3. Punch two or three holes in the left side of each pocket and the cover.
4. Fasten the book together using your choice of material as ties.
5. Glue the poem or information strips onto each pocket as shown on the overview pages of each book.

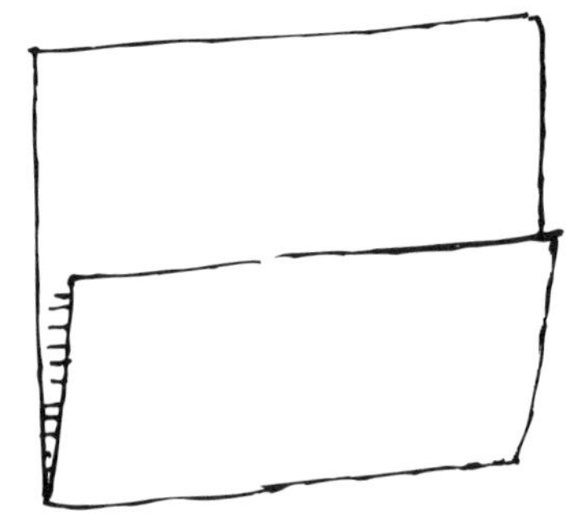

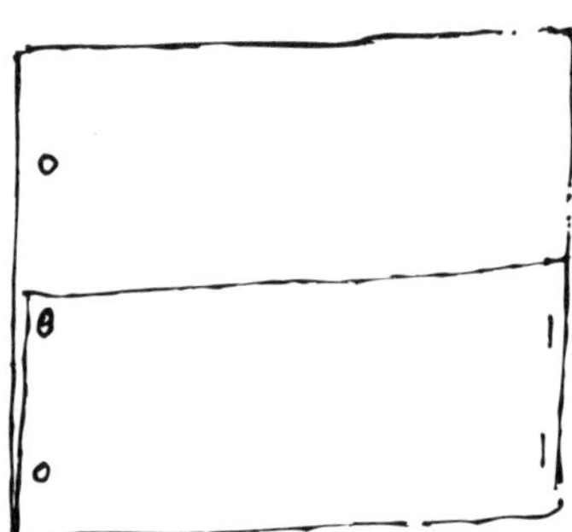

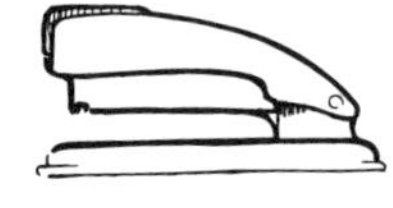

Valentine's Day

This joyful holiday book is built around a Valentine's poem. Students will experience art, oral and written language, and math.

Valentine's Day Book Overview pages 6 and 7
These pages show and tell what is in each pocket.

Cover Design ____________________ page 8

Pocket Projects ______________ pages 9–23
Step-by-step directions and patterns for the activities that go in each pocket.

Pocket Labels __________ pages 24 and 25
This poem can also be used for pocket chart activities throughout the month:

- Chant the poem
- Listen for rhyming words
- Learn new vocabulary
- Identify sight words
- Put words or lines in the correct order

Picture Dictionary ________________ page 26
Use the picture dictionary to introduce new vocabulary and as a spelling reference. Students can add new pictures, labels, and descriptive adjectives to the page as their vocabulary increases.

Writing Form ____________________ page 27
Use this form for story writing or as a place to record additional vocabulary words.

BIBLIOGRAPHY

Arthur's Valentine by Marc Brown; Little, Brown and Co., 1980.
Cranberry Valentine by Wende and Harry Devlin; Macmillan Publishing Co., 1986.
Four Valentines in a Rainstorm by Felicia Bond; HarperCollins Publishers, 1983.
It's Valentine's Day by Jack Prelutsky; Scholastic, 1983.
One Very Best Valentine's Day by Joan W. Blos; Simon & Schuster, 1990.
One Zillion Valentines by Frank Mondell; Mulberry Books, 1981.
A Valentine for Ms. Vanilla by Harriet Ziefert; Puffin Books, 1991.
The Valentine Bears by Eve Bunting; Houghton Mifflin, 1983.
Valentine's Day by Gail Gibbons; Holiday House, 1986.

POCKET 1

Cupid with Arrow and Bow **page 9**
Let students share what they know about this Valentine's Day figure. Provide them with additional facts as well. Then construct a charming 3-D Cupid from paper plates.

Cupid found love between... **page 10**
Tell students that one day Cupid decided to go out into the world to see how many places he could find love. Brainstorm and list students' ideas of situations where love can be found. Examples may range from common to unusual:

A grandmother and a grandfather
A boy and his dog
A baby and her blanket
The sun and a rainbow

Students name a situation of their choice and tell a bit about the relationship.

POCKET 2

Broken Heart Card **pages 11–13**
Talk about the meaning of the expression "to have a broken heart." "Can a heart really be broken? What does it mean if we say someone has a broken heart? Why would we use this symbol on a valentine card?" Students cut, fold, and glue to create a unique card to give to a favorite valentine.

Hugs & Kisses Graph **pages 14–17**
Students sort candy by color and design and then graph the results.

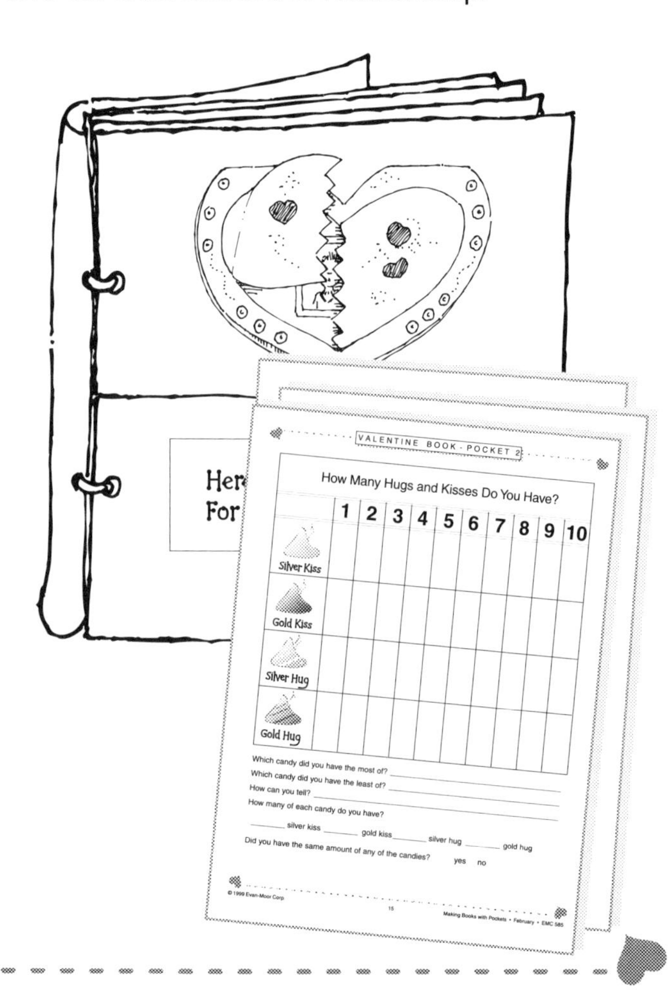

POCKET 3

Lovebirds **pages 18 and 19**
Students learn about lovebirds by reading information provided and make a pair of lovebirds from construction paper.

Things That Come in Pairs **page 20**
Before doing the activity, define the term "pair" (two things that belong together). Brainstorm with your class and list a few things that come in pairs. Divide into small groups so that students can benefit from combined brainpower when thinking of pairs of things. Each student should have a form on which to write the pairs their group thinks of. Compile the group lists into a longer class list. Challenge students to continue thinking of pairs to add to the list over the next few days. If desired, glue lists to larger pieces of construction paper.

POCKET 4

Tissue Paper Heart **pages 21 and 22**
Use a collage technique to create a pretty paper heart with a ruffle around the edge—a great gift for that special valentine.

Love Is... Stationery **page 23**
Students use the stationery to write a description of what love is (e.g., Love is... washing my dog on a hot day).

VALENTINE'S DAY BOOK COVER

Note: Reproduce this cover decoration for students to color, cut out, and glue to the cover of their Valentine books.

Cupid with Arrow and Bow

Materials

- 1½ small paper plates
- 6 cotton balls
- silver glitter
- pink pipe cleaners
- construction paper
  arrow—pink, four 2" (5 cm) pieces
  eyes—white and blue scraps
- 1 coffee stirrer
- paint
- marking pens
- glue
- scissors
- stapler

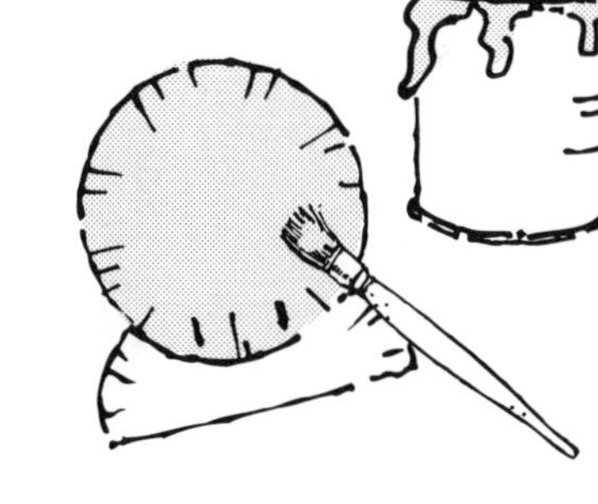

Steps to Follow

1. Staple half a plate to the whole paper plate.
2. Paint the paper plates.
3. Glue cotton balls to the top of head. String glue over the cotton and sprinkle with glitter.
4. Bend the pipe cleaner into the shape of a bow and twist the ends together.
5. Turn the coffee stirrer into an arrow by gluing on a point and feathers made from the pink construction paper.
6. Slip the arrow through the bow and glue both ends of the arrow to Cupid's body.
7. Add eyes cut from white and blue construction paper. Draw a mouth and a nose.

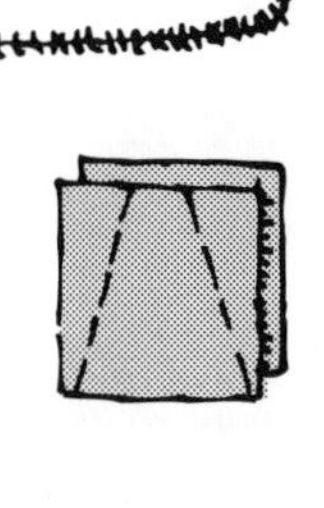

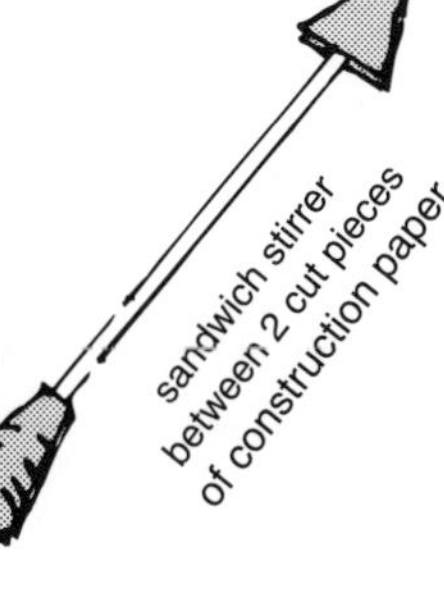

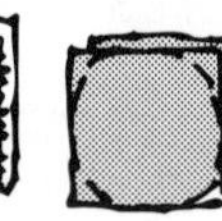

Name: ____

Cupid found love between ...

Broken Heart Card

Materials

- heart card pattern on page 12, reproduced on red paper
- broken heart pattern on page 13, reproduced on pink paper
- scissors
- glue
- marking pens
- sequins, glitter
- student photograph

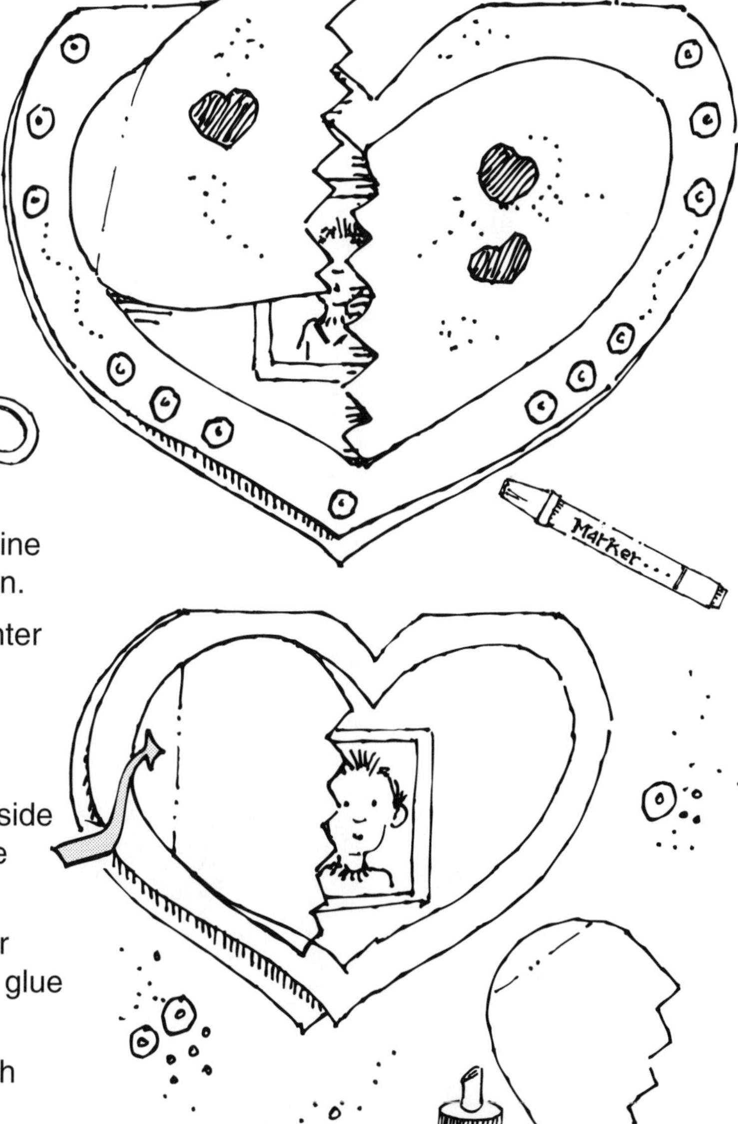

Steps to Follow

1. Cut out heart card pattern. Fold on line indicated and cut out marked section.
2. Glue the student's picture to the center of the heart.
3. Cut out the broken heart, making two pieces.
4. Fold each heart piece along the outside edge, forming a flap. Put glue on the back side of these folded sections.
5. Match the heart pieces with the inner heart outline drawn on the card and glue down the flaps.
6. Decorate the outside of the heart with markers, sequins, or glitter.
7. Write a personal message inside the card.

Heart Card Pattern

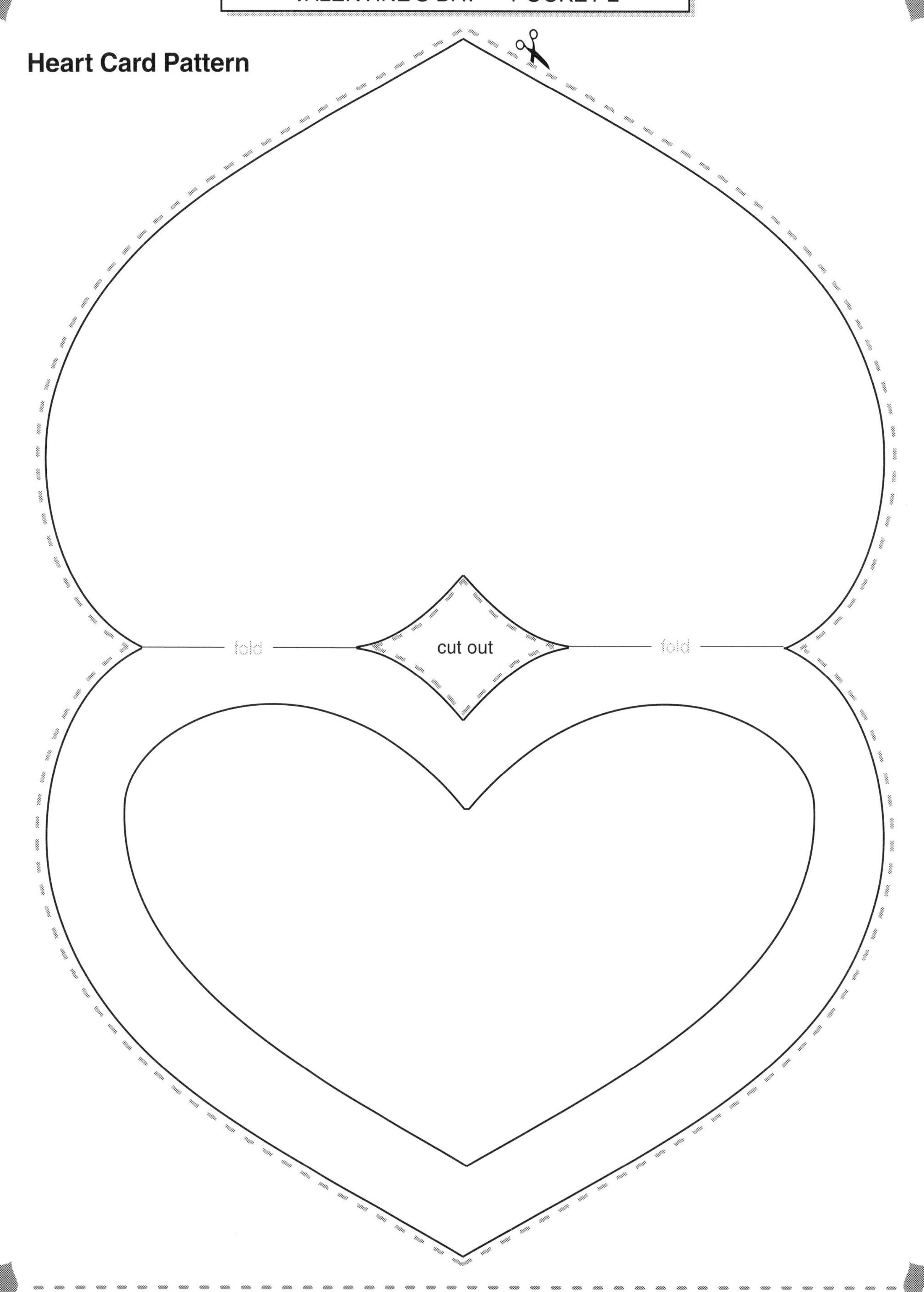

Broken Heart Card Pattern

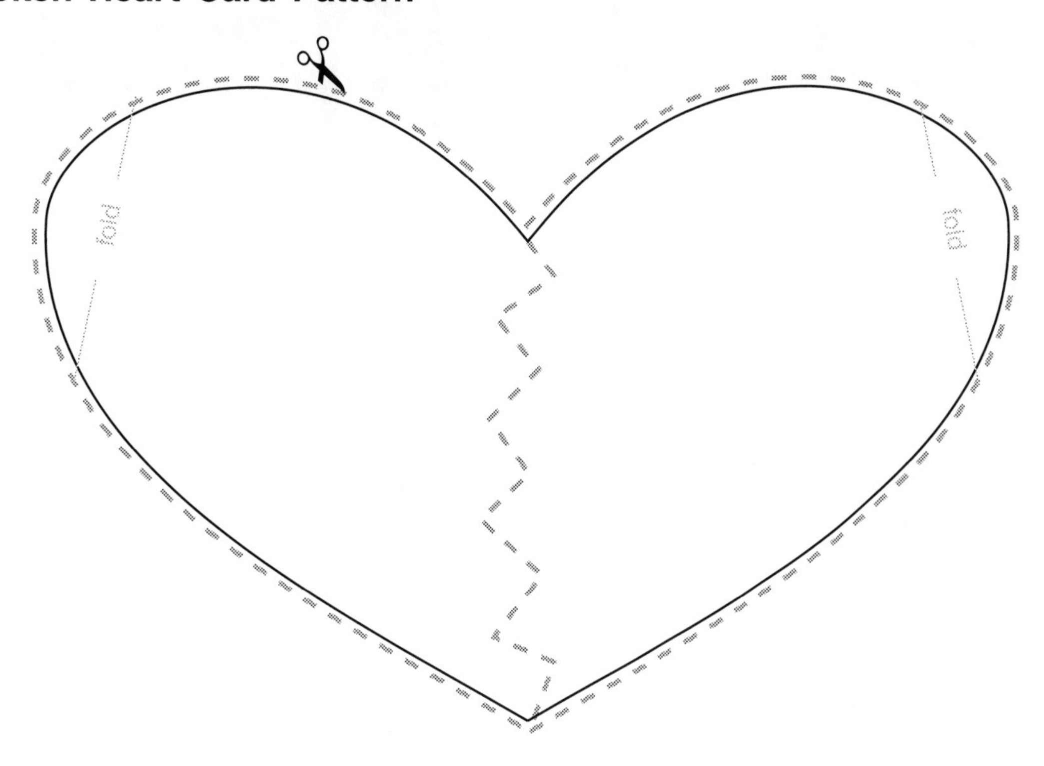

Broken Heart Card Pattern

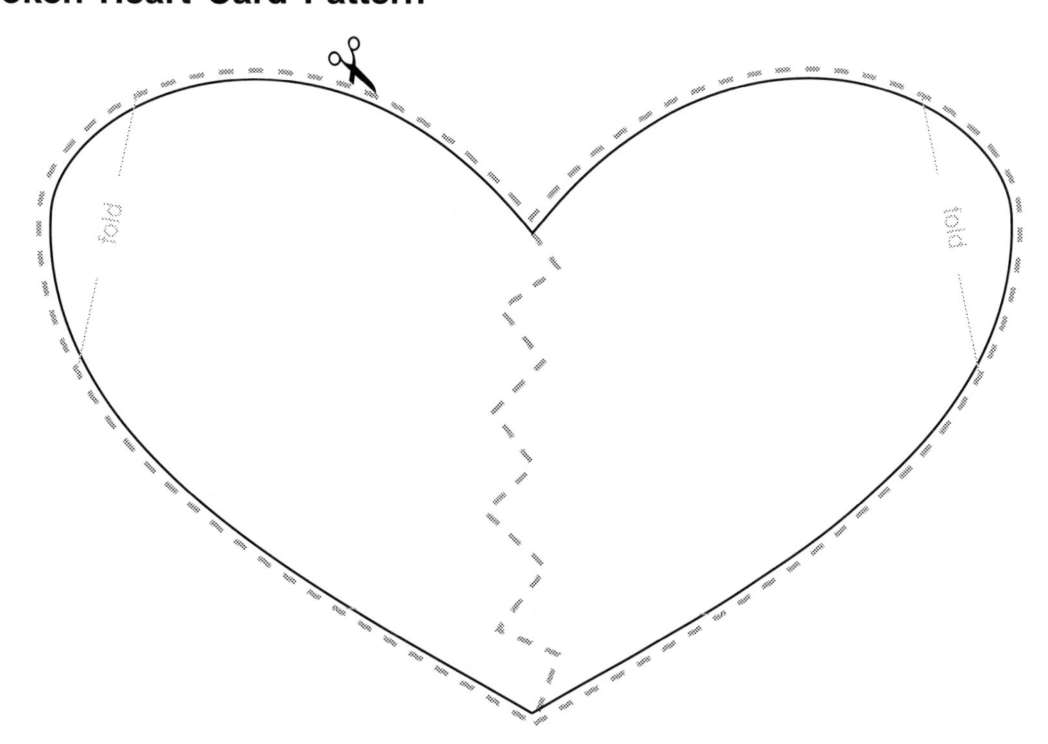

Hugs & Kisses

Math Graph

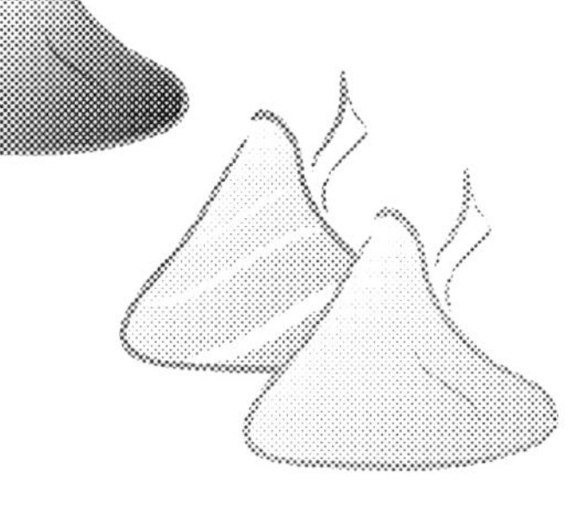

Materials

- Hershey's Hugs®—both plain and almond
- Hershey's Kisses®—both plain and almond
- reproduction of student graph, page 15
- reproduction of class tally, page 16
- reproduction of group graph, page 17
- crayons
- 1" x 6" (2.5 x 15 cm) paper strips

Steps to Follow

1. Mix up the four types of candy and give each student a handful.
2. Pose the question, "How many Hugs and Kisses do you have?"
3. Have the students sort the candy by color and design.
4. Complete the individual graph and questions (page 15). Each student's will be different.
5. Have each student add a tally mark to the class tally (page 16) for the type of candy he or she had the most of. (You may wish to enlarge the class tally or reproduce it on an overhead transparency.) Make observations of the chart together as a class. For example:

   _____ was the most common type of candy.

   _____ was the least common type of candy.

   _____ people had more of _____ candy than any other type of candy.

6. Complete the group graph. Mount a copy of page 17 on a larger piece of construction paper. Give each student one paper strip. Have each student add a paper chain link under the type of candy he or she prefers—Hugs or Kisses. (Staple links together.)

   Make observations about the finished graph. For example:

   _____ people like Hugs more than Kisses.

   _____ people like Kisses more than Hugs.

   More people like _____ than _____.

   Fewer people like _____ than _____.

How Many Hugs and Kisses Do You Have?

	1	2	3	4	5	6	7	8	9	10
Silver Kiss										
Gold Kiss										
Silver Hug										
Gold Hug										

Which candy did you have the most of? ______________________________

Which candy did you have the least of? ______________________________

How can you tell? ______________________________

How many of each candy do you have?

________ silver kiss ________ gold kiss ________ silver hug ________ gold hug

Did you have the same amount of any of the candies? yes no

Class Tally of the Most Common Candy

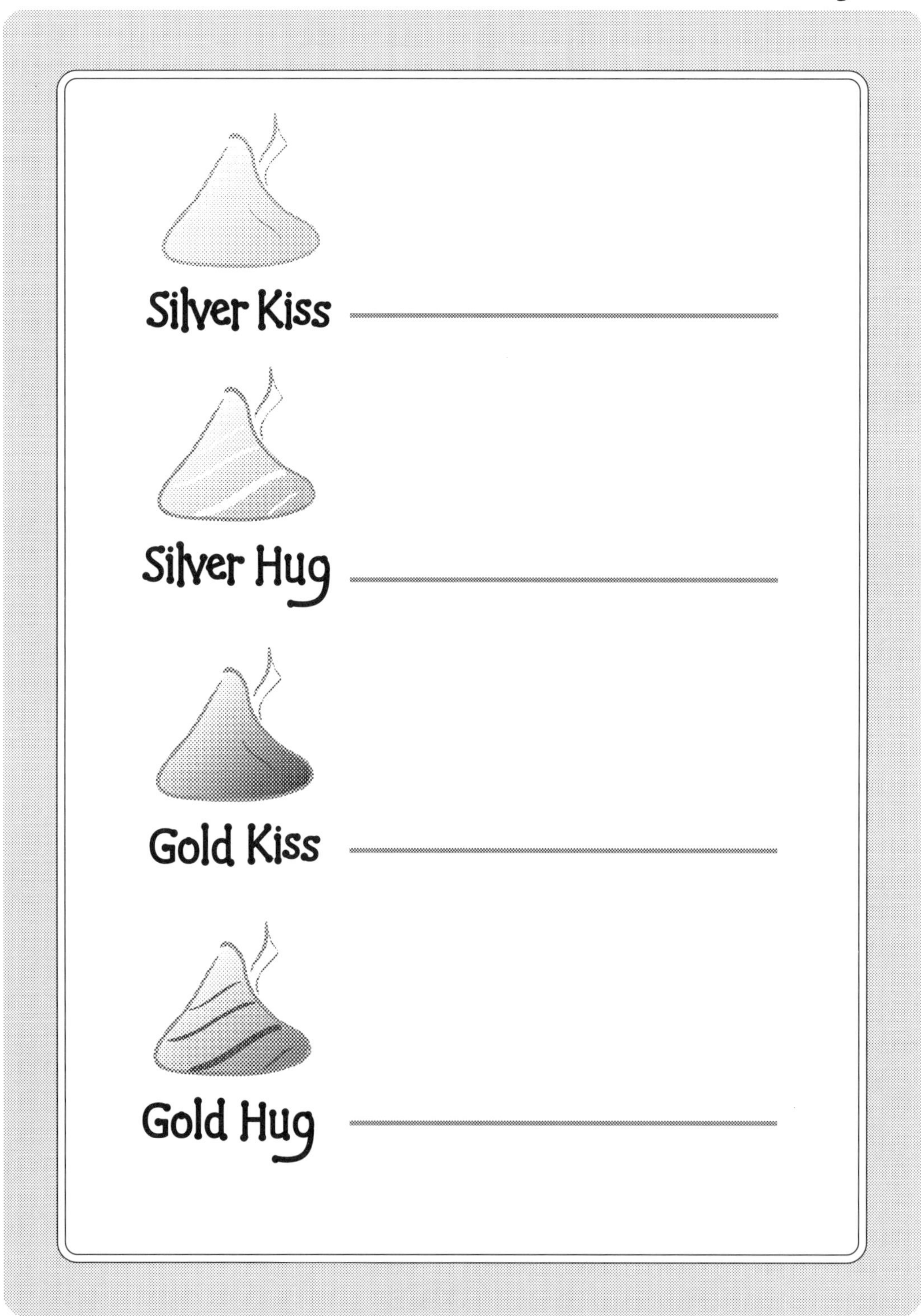

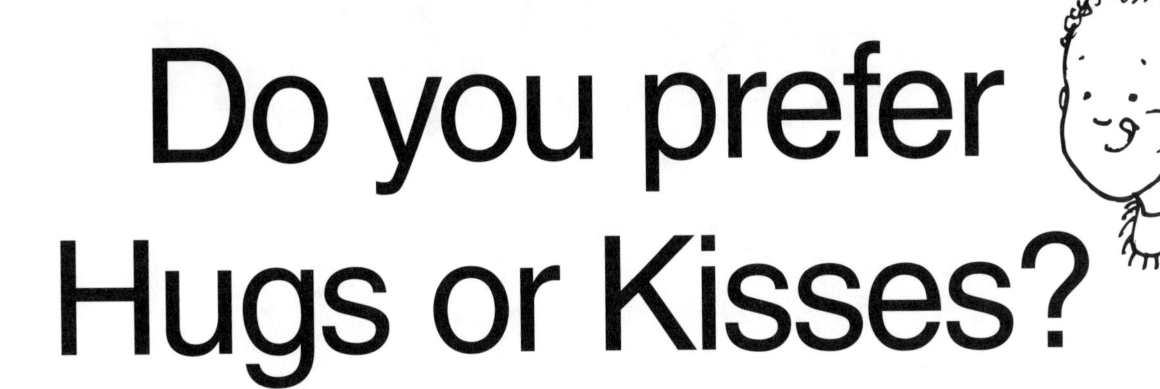

Do you prefer Hugs or Kisses?

Hugs	Kisses

Lovebirds

Materials

- construction paper
  patterns on page 19, reproduced on light green
  lower body—dark green, 3" x 4" (7.5 x 10 cm)
  heart—red, 5" (13 cm)
- marking pens
- scissors
- glue

Steps to Follow

1. Share with students the information about lovebirds provided on page 19.
2. Cut out lovebirds and the information.
3. Round dark green paper as shown to create lower body.
4. Glue dark green body section behind light green section.
5. Add details with marking pens—eyes, beak, feathers.
6. Fold red square in half and cut a heart. (You may want young students to practice with scrap paper first.)
7. Glue lovebirds to heart with beaks touching.
8. Glue the information about lovebirds on the back of the birds.

Information Cards

Lovebirds are small parrots. They are called lovebirds because they show great affection for their mates. Lovebirds are found in Africa, Asia, and South America. They are mostly green or light gray. Some people keep lovebirds as pets.

When two people show that they like each other very much, others may call them lovebirds.

Lovebird Patterns

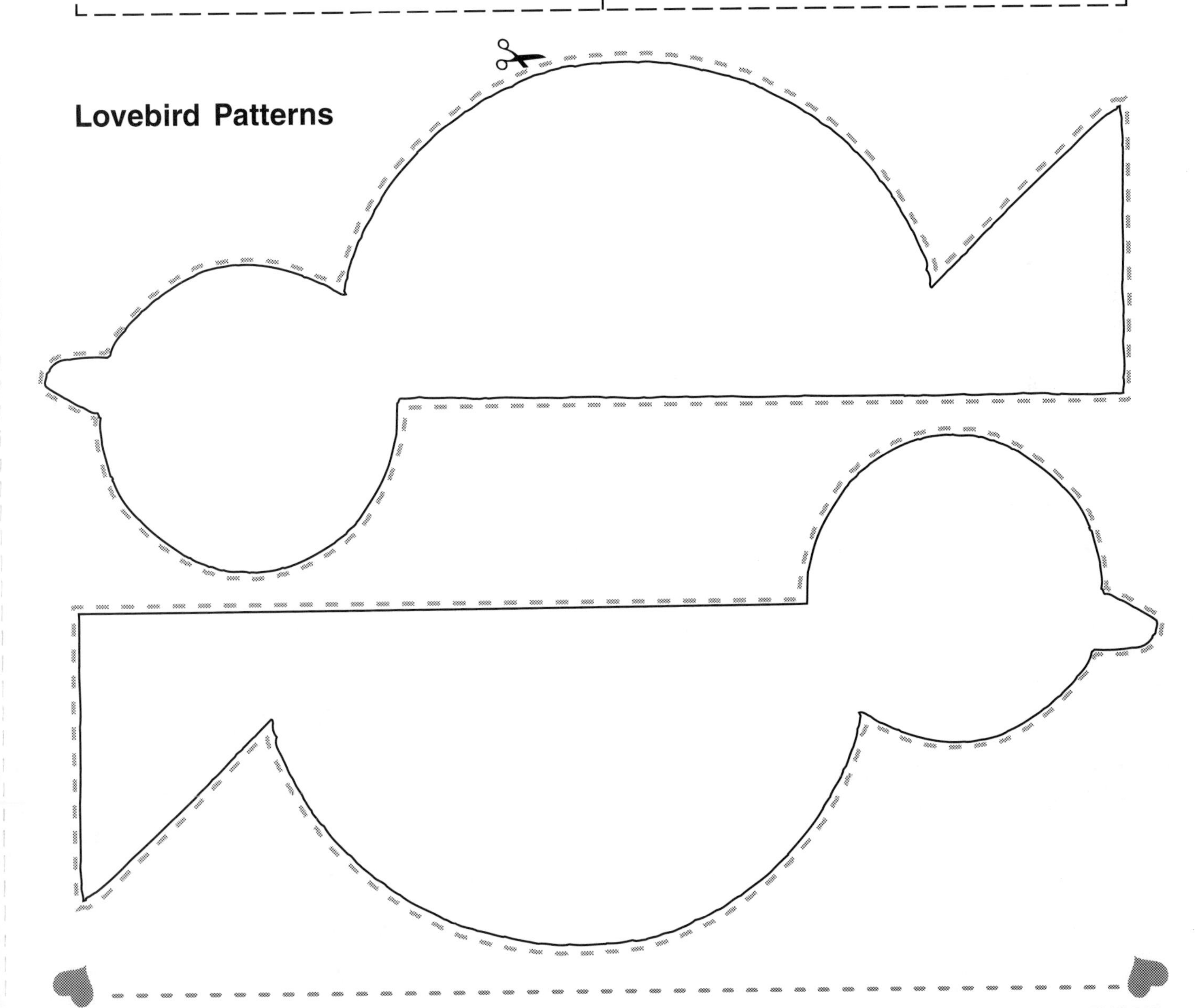

Things That Come in Pairs

Things That Come in Pairs

Tissue Paper Heart

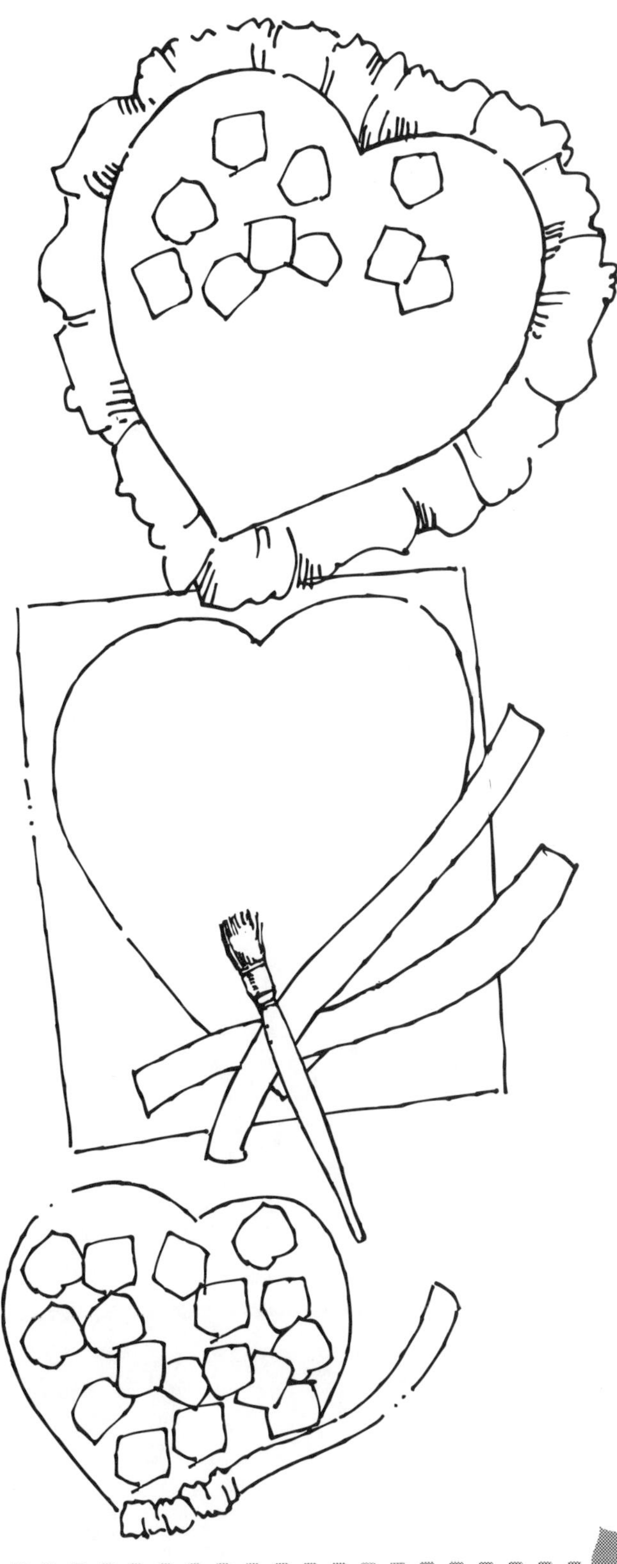

Materials

- heart pattern on page 22, reproduced on white construction paper
- strips of red, pink, and dark pink tissue paper
- 2" (5 cm) wide strips of lavender tissue paper
- starch
- paintbrush
- scissors
- glue

Steps to Follow

1. Paint starch on the white heart.
2. Use scraps of tissue paper to decorate the heart. Scraps can be cut into squares or torn in free-form shapes. Lay the scraps on the wet starch.
3. Paint over with starch. Let dry.
4. Cut out heart.
5. Use lavender strips of tissue paper to create a ruffled edge. Spread glue along a section of the edge of the heart. Fold and pleat tissue paper as you attach it to the edge. Apply glue to another section and repeat.

Heart Pattern

Love is...

Note: Reproduce this page and page 25 to label each of the four pockets of the Valentine book.

Pocket 1

Here is Cupid
With his arrow and bow,

Pocket 2
Here is a Valentine card
For someone I know.

Pocket 3

Here are two lovebirds
Who will never part.

Pocket 4

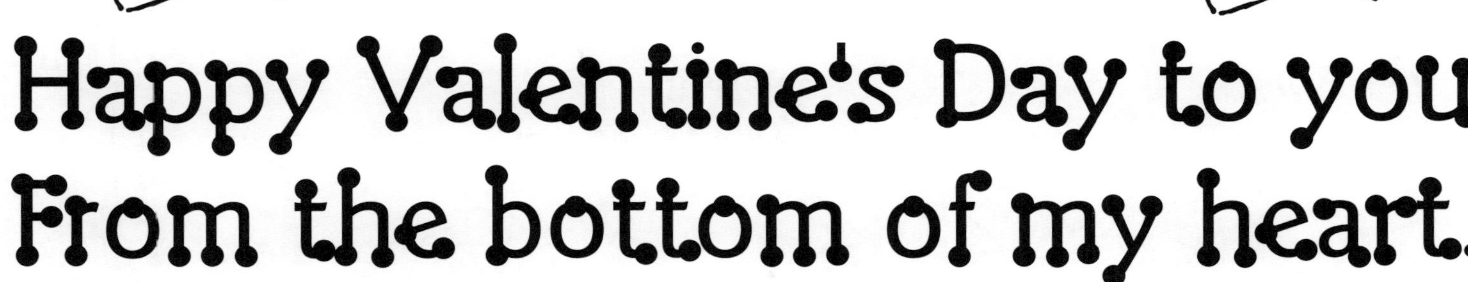

Happy Valentine's Day to you
From the bottom of my heart.

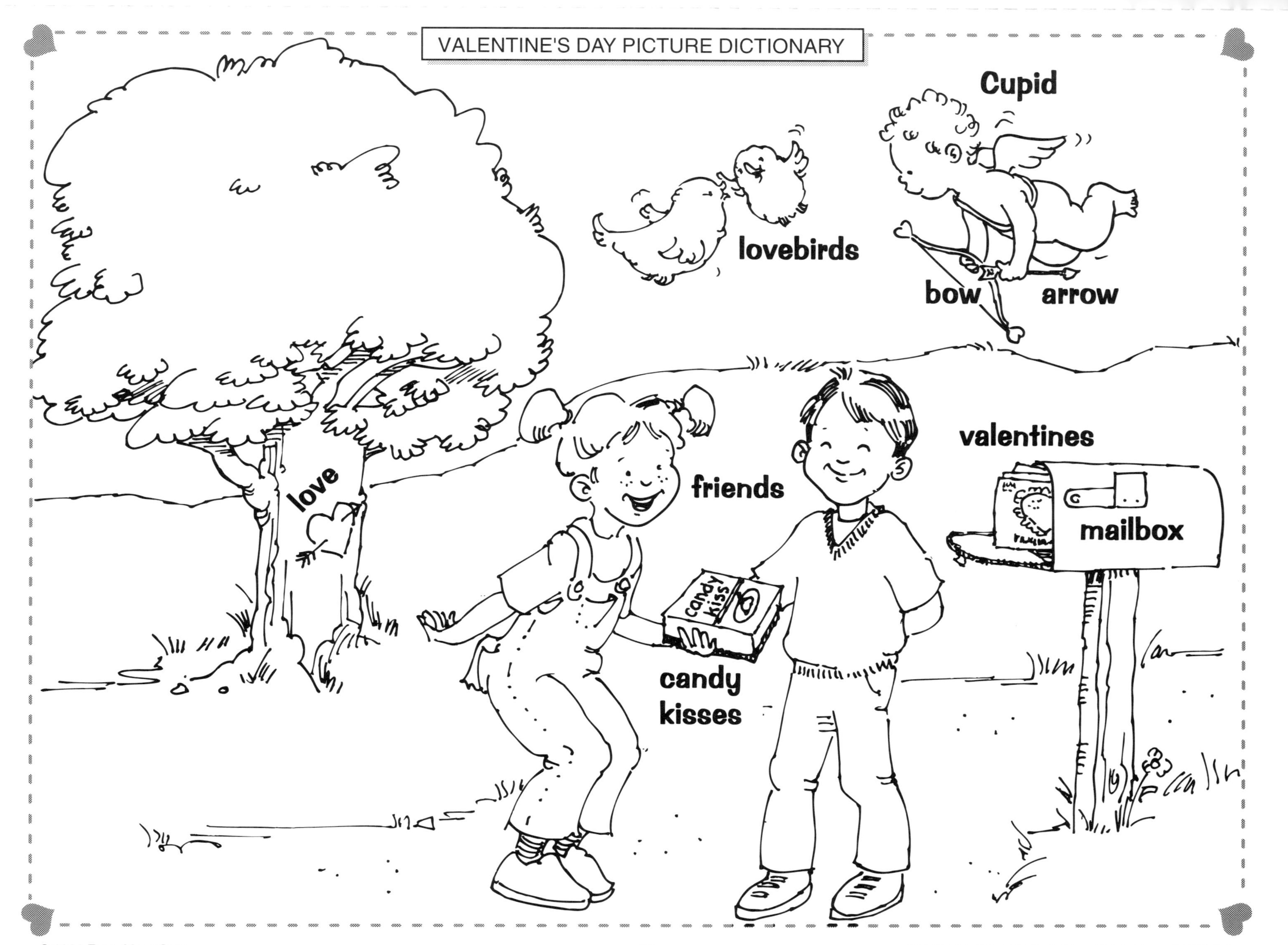
VALENTINE'S DAY PICTURE DICTIONARY
Cupid
lovebirds
bow
arrow
love
friends
valentines
mailbox
candy kiss
candy kisses

VALENTINE'S DAY WRITING FORM

Name: ______________________________

Two Great Presidents

This five-pocket book celebrates two famous presidents—George Washington and Abraham Lincoln. You'll enrich your social studies curriculum and involve students in recording factual information and creating original writing.

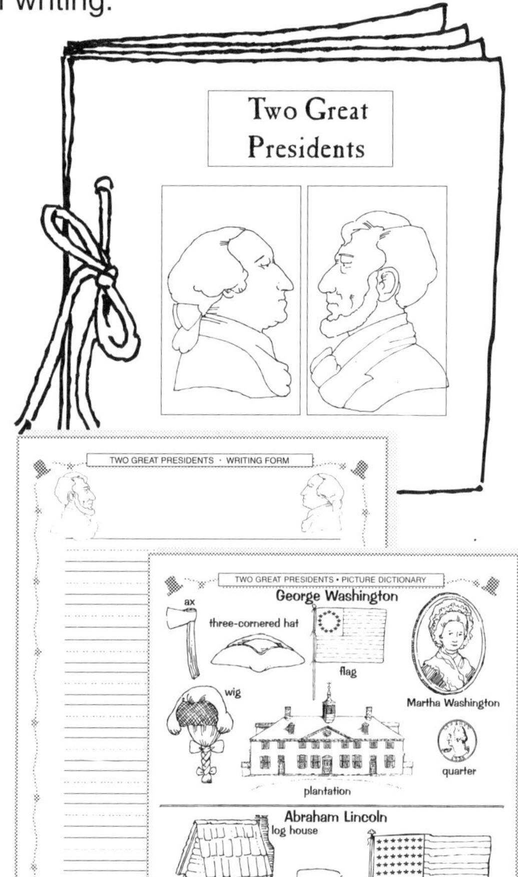

BIBLIOGRAPHY

Abe Lincoln's Hat by Martha Brenner; Scholastic, 1994.
Abraham Lincoln by Kathie Billingslea Smith; Simon & Schuster, 1987.
George Washington by Kathie Billingslea Smith; Simon & Schuster, 1987.
George Washington: A Picture Book Biography by James Cross Giblin; Scholastic, 1992.
Honest Abe by Edith Kunhardt; Greenwillow Books, 1993.
If You Grew Up with Abraham Lincoln by Ann McGovern; Scholastic, 1982.
If You Grew Up with George Washington by Ruth Belov Gross; Scholastic, 1982.
Just a Few Words, Mr. Lincoln: The Story of the Gettysburg Address by Jean Fritz; Scholastic, 1993.
A Picture Book of Abraham Lincoln by David A. Adler; Holiday House, 1989.
A Picture Book of George Washington by David A. Adler; Holiday House, 1989.

POCKET 1

George Washington **pages 32 and 33**

Read books about our first president. List important facts on a chart. Share illustrations and talk about the clothing styles of the times to prepare students for this art project during which they make George Washington from construction paper.

If I Were... **page 34**

Talk about what a change it was for the new country of the United States of America to have a president after being ruled by a king. Tell students to pretend they have just been elected presidents of brand new countries. Their jobs are to help plan what the countries will be like—what laws (rules) will they make, what will the flag look like, etc. Conduct as much discussion as is needed to prepare your students to complete the worksheet.

POCKET 2

Quarter Book **pages 35–37**

A picture of the "Father of Our Country" is found on both the quarter and the one-dollar bill. Students will make a book that looks like a quarter and complete it using one of the writing suggestions on page 35.

POCKET 3

Abraham Lincoln **pages 38 and 39**
After learning about the sixteenth president, students make Lincoln from construction paper.

Honest Abe's Hat **pages 40–44**
Learn why Abe's hat was special, make a top hat, and use one of a number of writing suggestions provided.

POCKET 4

Penny Book **pages 45–47**
Lincoln's picture is found on both the penny and the five-dollar bill. Students will make a book that looks like a penny and complete it using one of the writing suggestions on page 45.

POCKET 5

A Different Time
A Different Place **pages 48–50**
After reading about life during the times of George Washington and Abraham Lincoln, students record information in two little books that go in this pocket.

TWO GREAT PRESIDENTS BOOK COVER

Note: Reproduce these cover decorations for students to color, cut out, and glue to the cover of their Two Great Presidents books.

Two Great Presidents

George Washington

Abraham Lincoln

George Washington

Materials

- tagboard templates made from patterns on page 33
- construction paper
  hat—red, 8" x 4" (20 x 10 cm)
  hair—white, 6" x 3" (15 x 7.5 cm)
  face—manila, 5" x 4 ½" (13 x 11.5 cm)
  shoulders—dark blue, 3" x 7 ½" (7.5 x 19 cm)
  eyes—scraps of white and black
- white tissue paper, 3" x 4" (7.5 x 10 cm)
- star stickers
- scissors
- glue
- marking pens

Steps to Follow

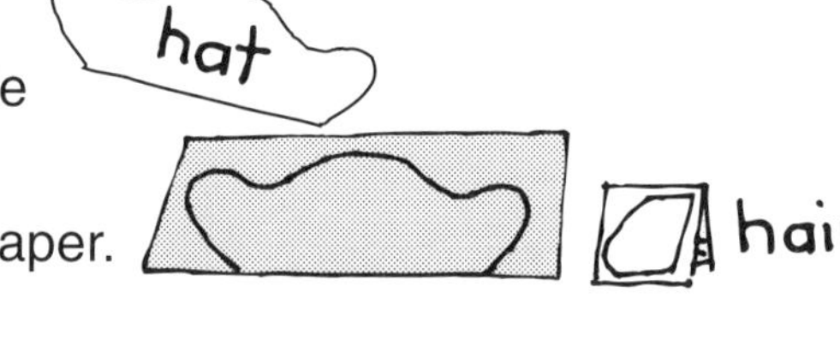

1. Using templates, cut out the hat from red construction paper. Cut 2 sections of hair from white construction paper.
2. Make the face by rounding one end of the manila paper.
3. Make the shoulders by rounding one long side of blue paper.
4. Glue the hair to both sides of the face. Glue on the hat.
5. Round off two corners of the white tissue paper. Glue the tissue paper to the shoulders around the neck, gathering it to create a ruffle.
6. Glue the head onto the shoulders.
7. Cut out eyes from scraps of white and black construction paper.
8. Add other facial features with marking pens. Add star stickers to the hat.

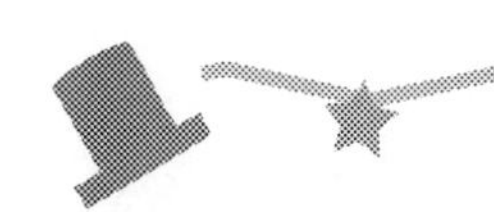

Washington's Hat and Hair Patterns

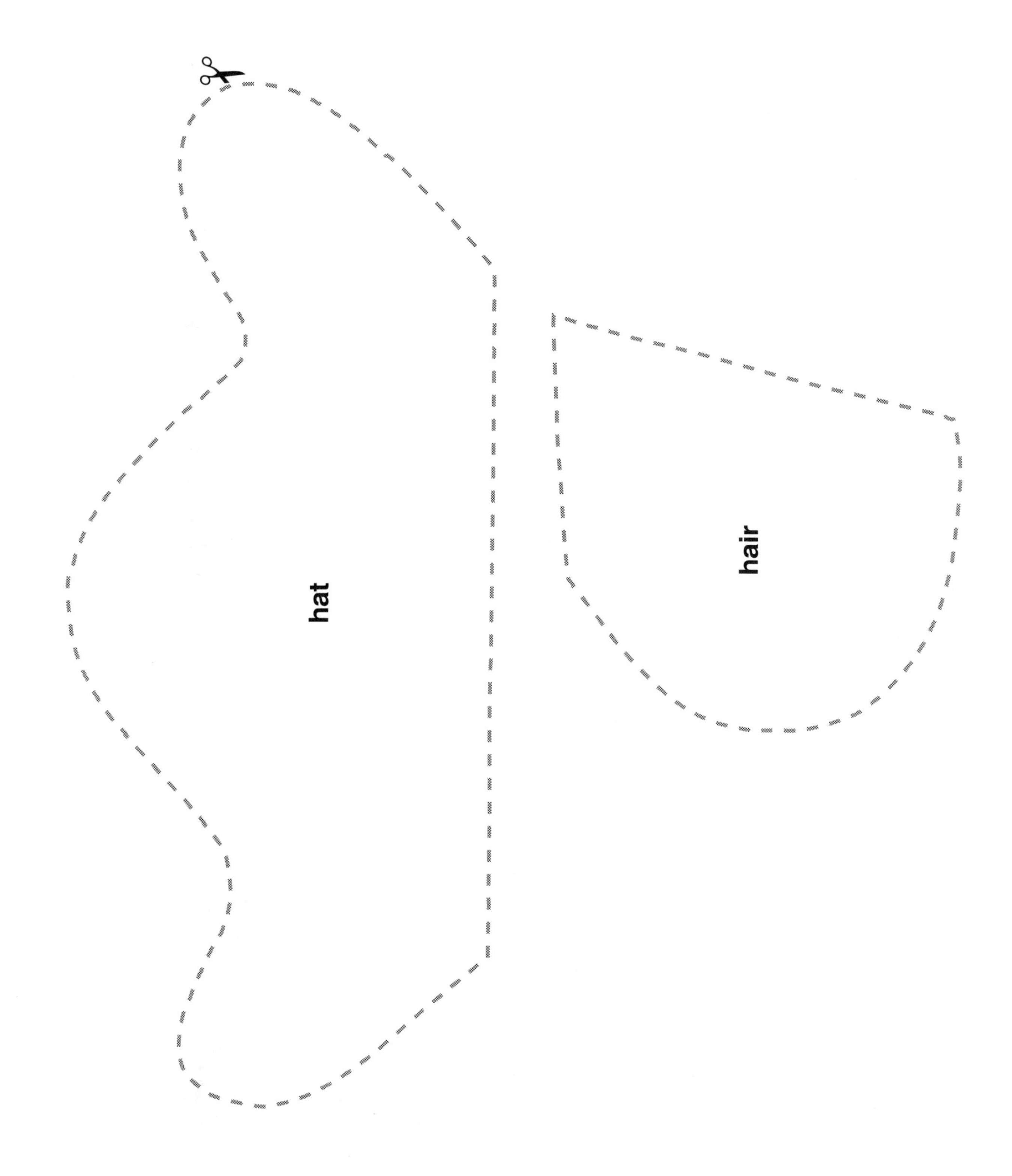

If I were the President of a new country...

The rules would be...

The flag would look like this...

Because ...

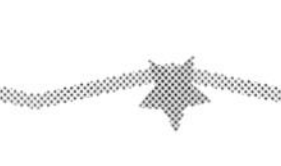

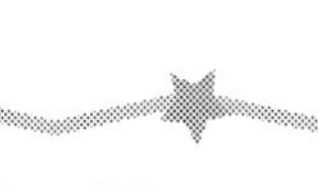

Quarter Book

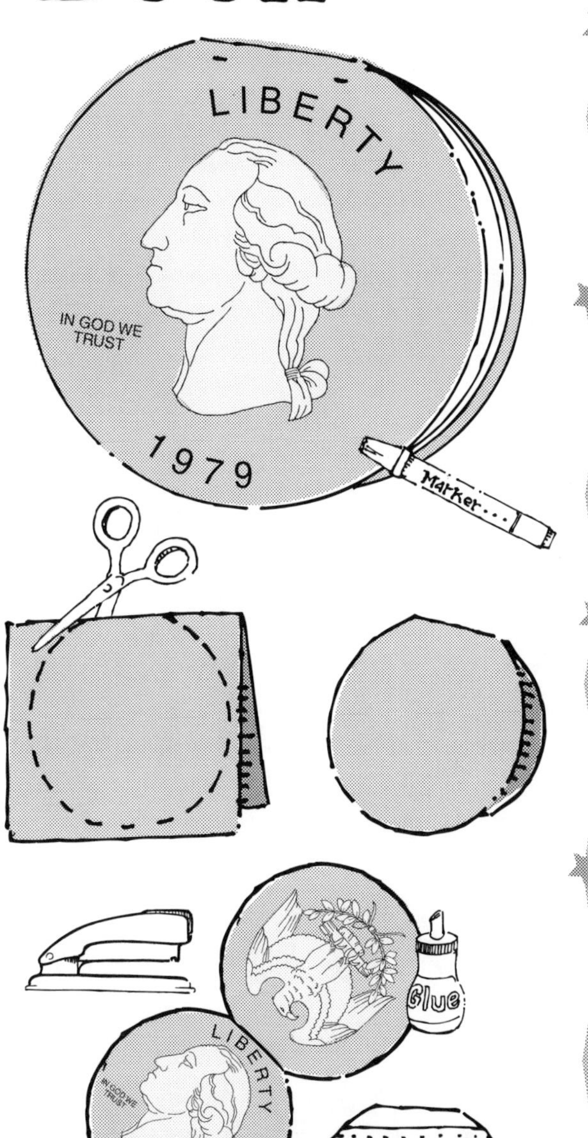

Materials

- tagboard template made from the circle pattern on page 36
- construction paper
  cover—gray, 12" x 18" (30.5 x 45.5 cm)
  coin patterns on page 37, reproduced on light blue
- scissors
- glue
- black marker
- writing paper
- stapler

Steps to Follow

1. Fold the gray paper in half.
2. Trace the circle template so that it slightly overlaps the fold.
3. Cut out the circle.
4. Cut out the head and tail patterns and glue one on each side of the book. Make sure both tops face the fold.
5. Use the marker to write the words from a United States quarter on each side.
6. Cut writing paper using the circle template.
7. Staple writing paper into the quarter book.

Writing Suggestions

1. Make a vocabulary book of words from the time period in which Washington lived.
2. Write about important events in Washington's life.
3. Write math problems that involve quarters.

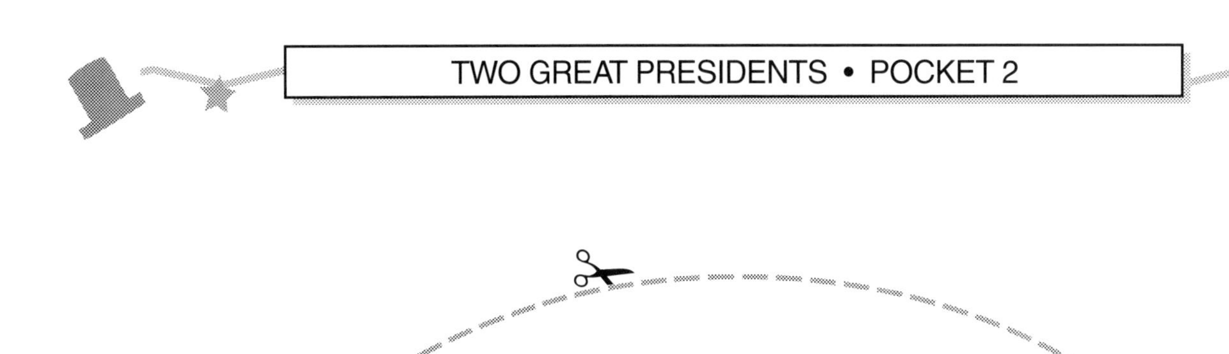

circle
template

Coin Patterns

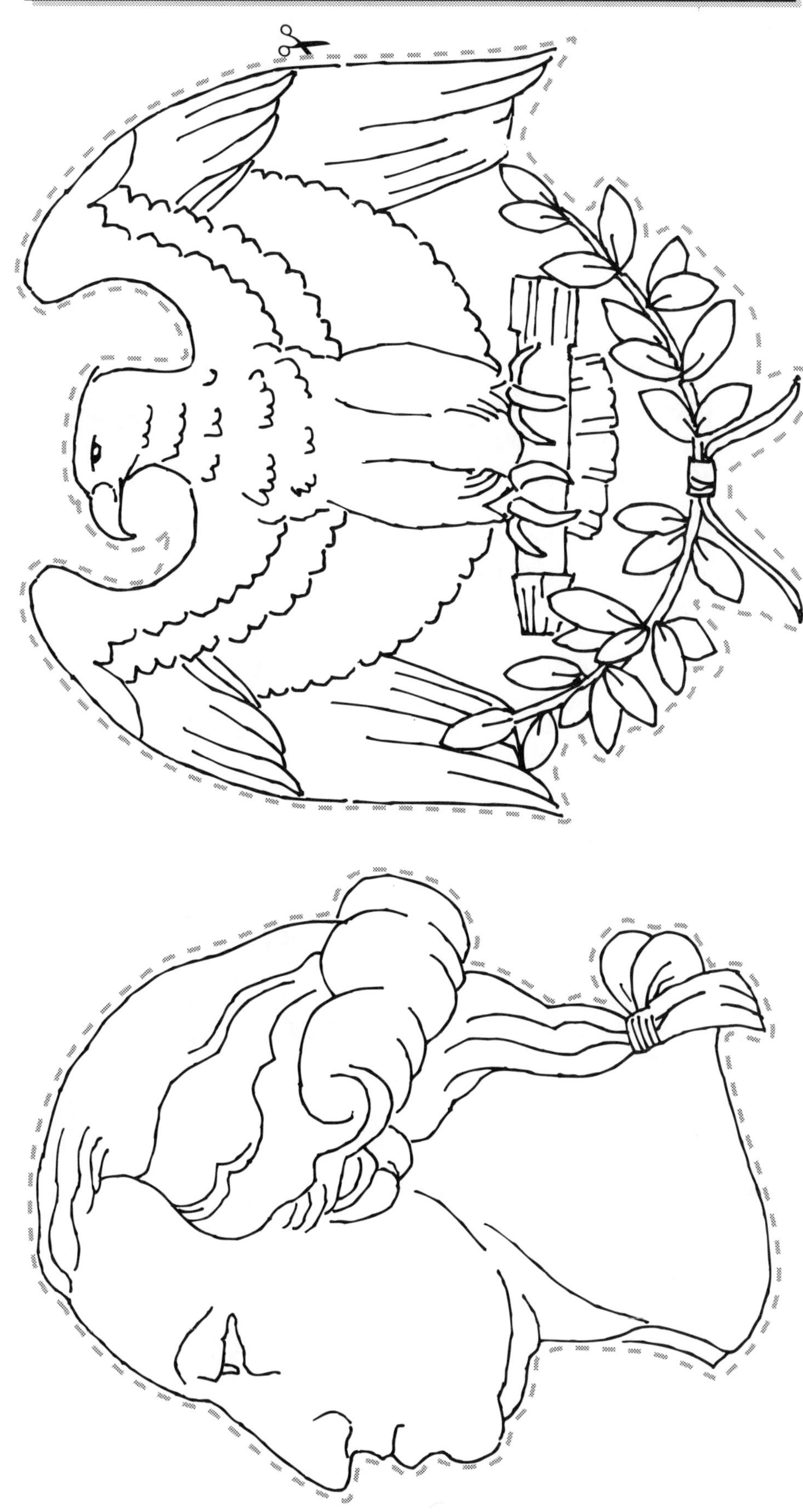

Abraham Lincoln

Materials

- tagboard templates made from the patterns on page 39
- construction paper
  hat—black, 6" x 5" (15 x 13 cm)
  brim—black, 7" x 1½" (18 x 4 cm)
  bow tie—black, 3" (7.5 cm) square
  face—manila, 5" x 4½" (13 x 11.5 cm)
  beard—brown, 6" (15 cm) square
  eyes—scraps of white and black
- scissors
- glue
- marking pens

Steps to Follow

1. Glue the black strip to the large black rectangle to make the top hat.
2. Round one end of the manila rectangle to form the face.
3. Use the tagboard templates to trace the beard and bow tie onto construction paper. Cut them out.
4. Glue the beard to the face. Glue on the bow tie and the hat.
5. Cut the eyes from scraps. Add other facial features with marking pens.

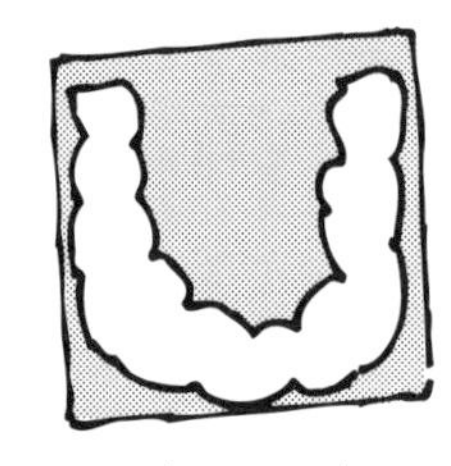

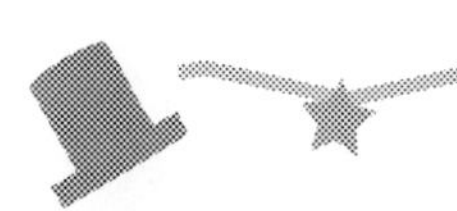

Lincoln's Bow Tie and Beard Patterns

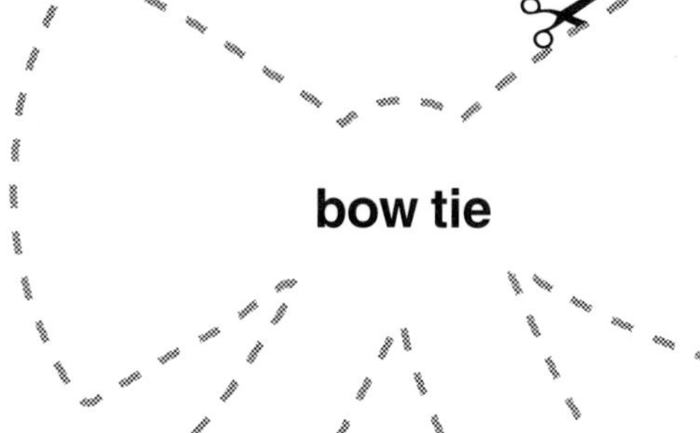

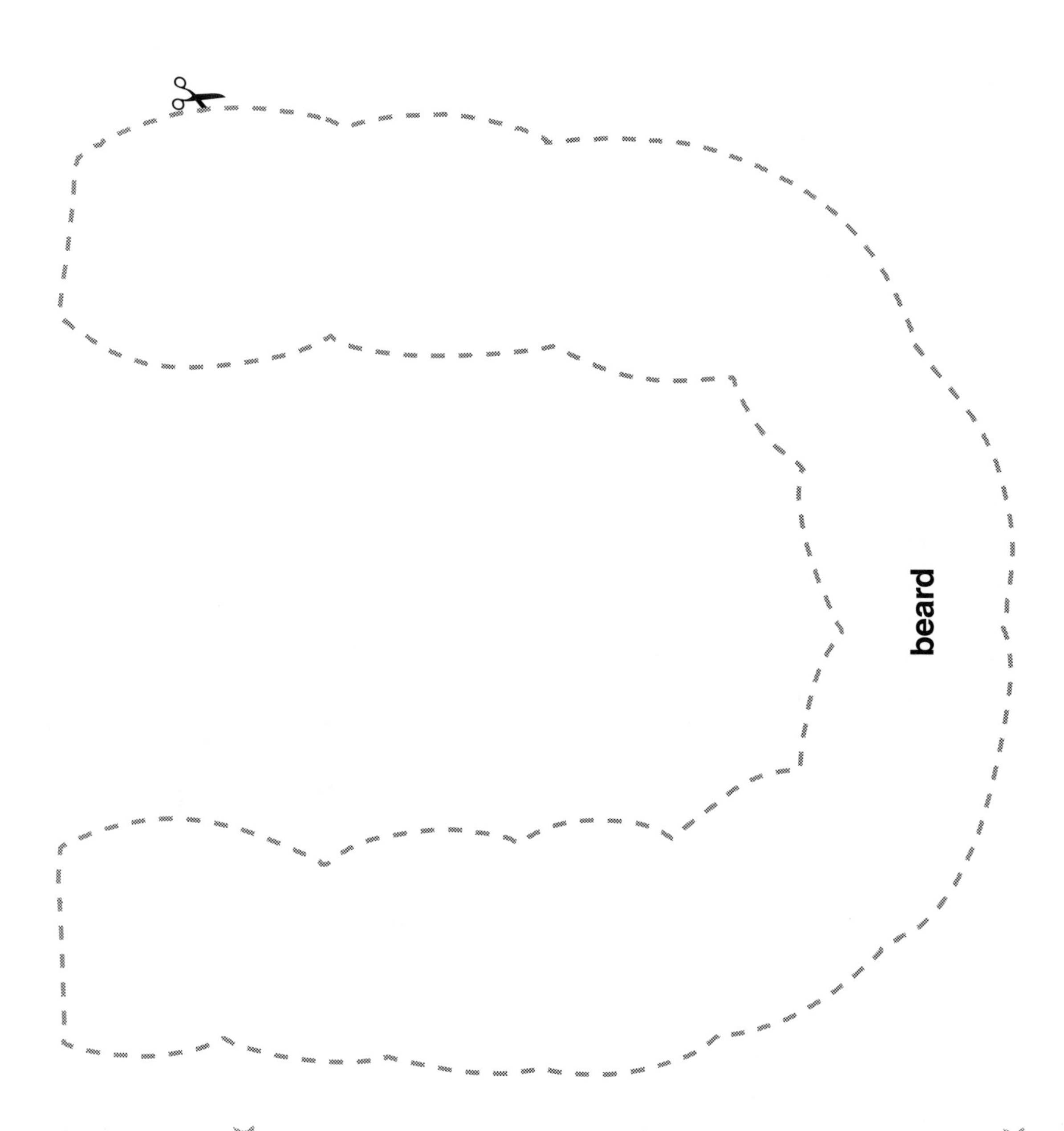

Honest Abe's Hat

Abraham Lincoln used his top hat to carry papers just like many people today use a briefcase. Make a hat to hold important papers about Abraham Lincoln. The next page gives teaching ideas for writing activities to put in the hat. Accompanying writing forms are on pages 42–44.

Read *Abe Lincoln's Hat* (see bibliography, page 28) to find out more about Abe's hat.

Materials

- construction paper
  brim—black, 10" x 6" (25.5 x 15 cm)
  hat body—black, 12" x 7" (30.5 x 18 cm)
- glue

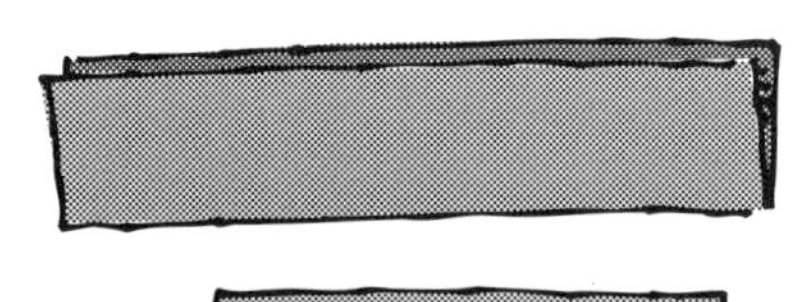

Steps to Follow

1. Fold the smaller black rectangle in half lengthwise to create the brim of the hat.
2. Open the brim and place one narrow end of the larger black rectangle against the crease. Glue across the bottom flap of the hat brim and refold.
3. Flip the hat over and you will have a pocket in the brim to hold important papers.

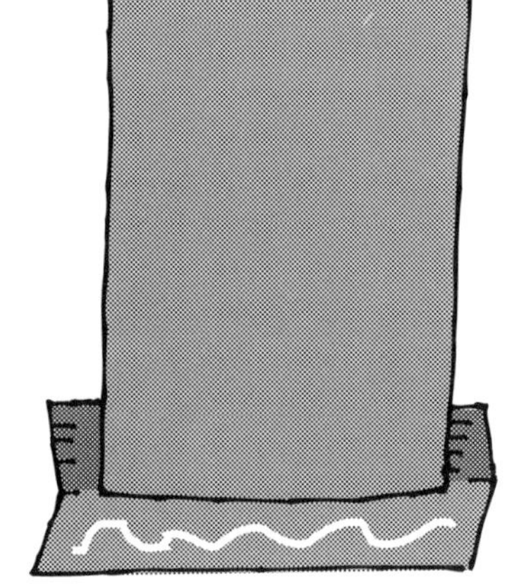

Writing Ideas for
Abe Lincoln's Hat

Here are some writing prompts you might use to create interesting papers to "carry" in the top hat you made.

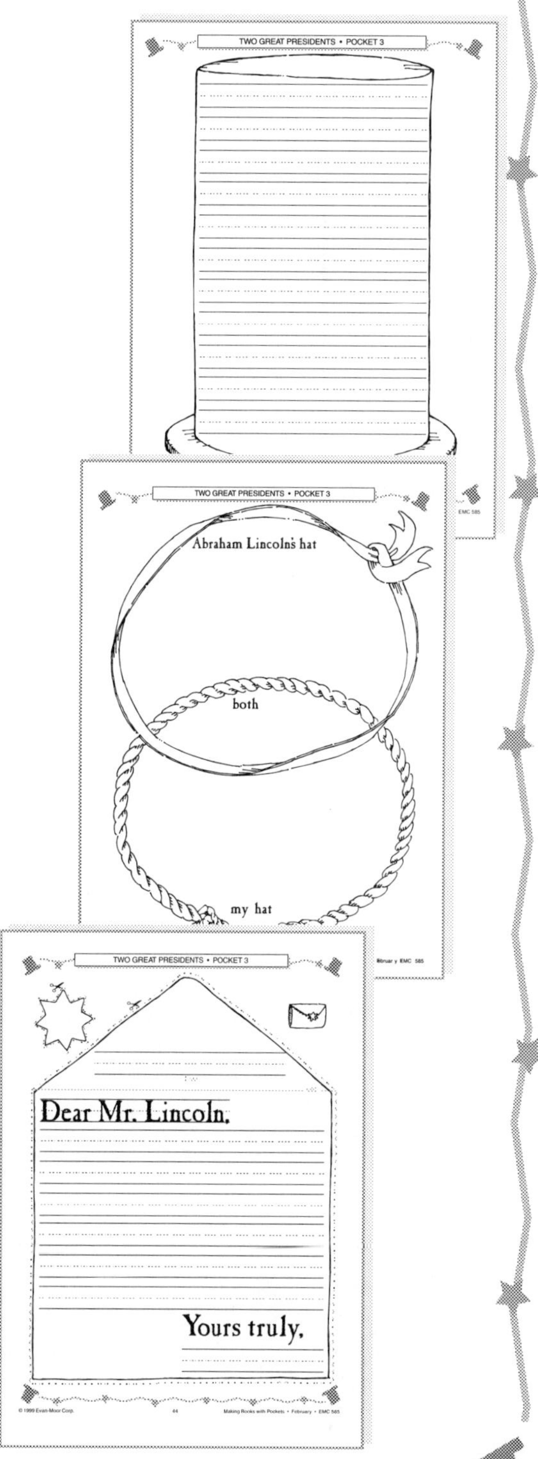

Hat Writing Form, page 42

1. Write true facts about Abraham Lincoln's hat.
   What material was it made of?
   Why was it also called a stovepipe hat?
   What special use did he have for the hat?

2. Write a story about a day Abe's hat rolled away.

3. Abraham Lincoln was often called "Honest Abe."
   Describe examples of honesty. Start your list with:
   Honesty is when....

4. The opposite of honest is dishonest.
   Fill the hat with as many pairs of opposites
   as you can. *For example: tall/short, day/night.*

Venn Diagram, page 43

Compare your hat with Abraham Lincoln's hat.
Think about shape, size, color, purpose, material.

Letter Writing Form, page 44

Write a letter to Abraham Lincoln thanking him for the important things he did for America.

Abraham Lincoln's hat
both
my hat

Date
fold
Dear Mr. Lincoln,
Yours truly,

Penny Book

Materials

- tagboard template made from the circle pattern on page 46
- construction paper
  cover—dark brown, 15" x 8" (38 x 20 cm)
  coin patterns on page 47, reproduced on light brown
- scissors
- glue
- black marker
- writing paper

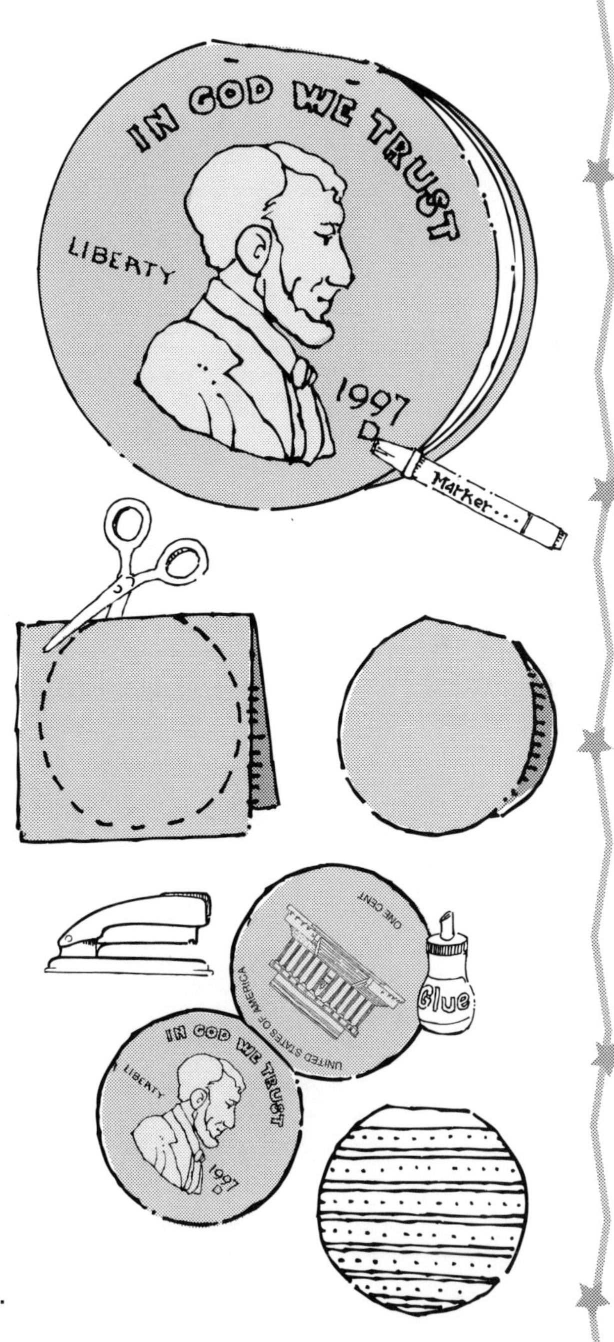

Steps to Follow

1. Fold the brown paper in half.
2. Trace the circle template so that it slightly overlaps the fold.
3. Cut out the circle.
4. Cut out the head and tail pictures and glue one on each side of the book. Make sure both tops face the fold.
5. Use the marker to write the words from a United States penny on each side.
6. Cut writing paper using the circle template.
7. Staple writing paper into the penny book.

Writing Suggestions

1. Make a vocabulary book of words from the time period in which Lincoln lived.
2. Write about important events in Lincoln's life.
3. Write math problems that involve pennies.

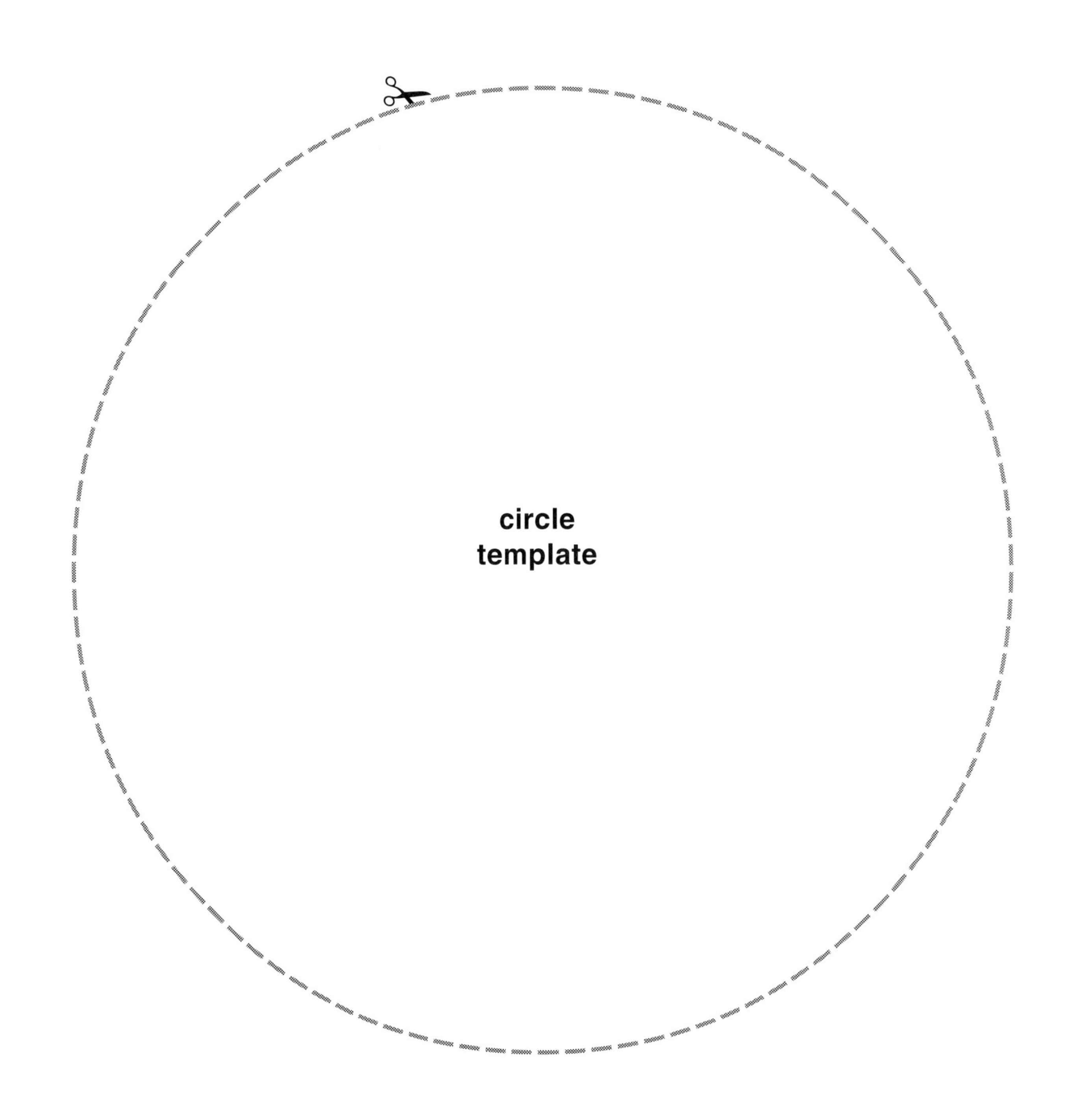

circle
template

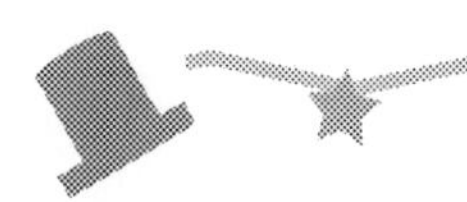

Coin Patterns

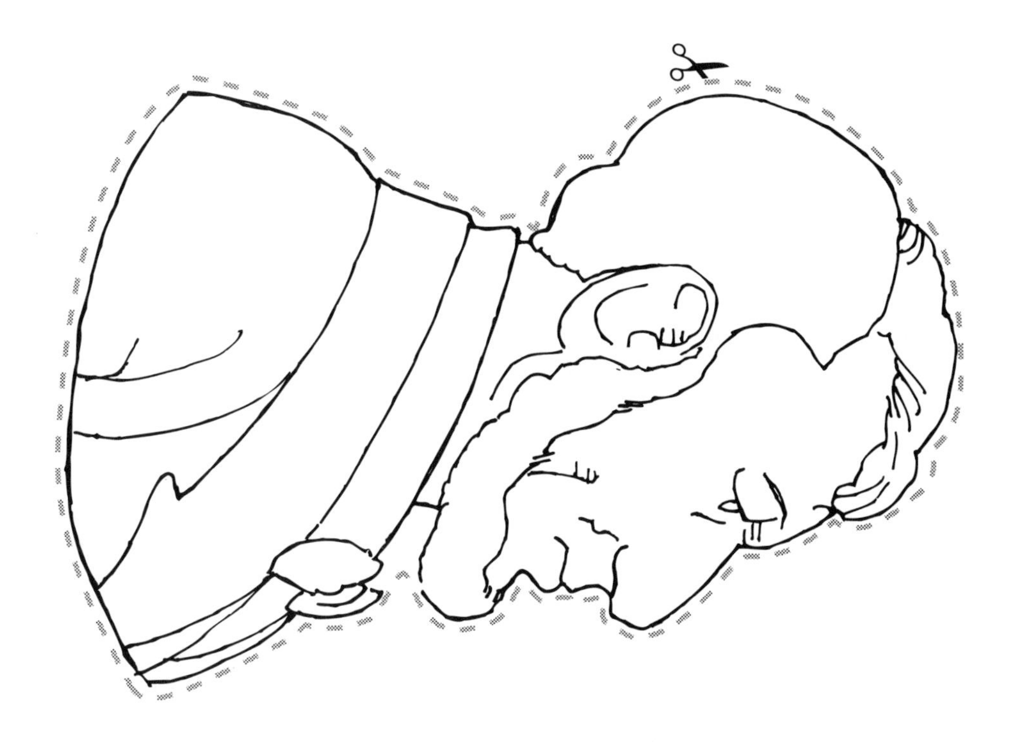

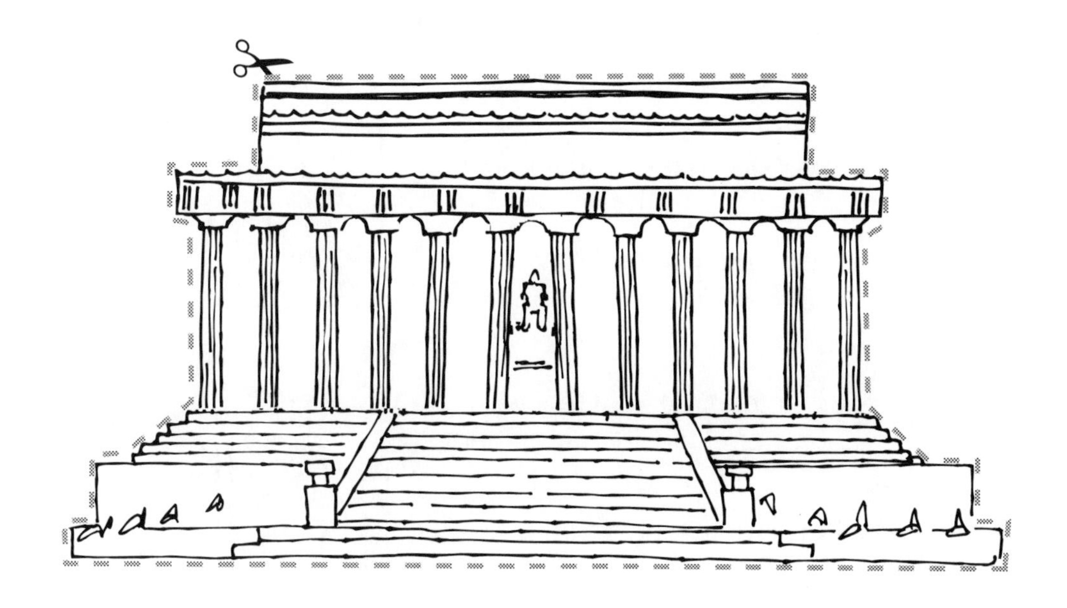

A Different Time A Different Place

Materials

- titles for book covers, page 49
- writing and drawing form on page 50 (7 pages for each book)
- two 9" x 18" (23 x 45.5 cm) pieces of construction paper for covers
- crayons
- pencils
- glue

Two Books of Facts

A Different Time
A Different Place
The Early 1800s

Different Time
Different Place
Colonial Times

Steps to Follow

To make each book:

1. Fold the construction paper in half to make a cover for the book.
2. Staple seven writing/drawing forms inside each cover.
3. Cut out the book titles and glue one onto each cover.

To write the books:

1. Read about life during the times of George Washington and Abraham Lincoln in a number of books.
2. Choose important facts on a single topic to write on each page (food, clothing, occupations, schooling, homes, etc.). For younger students, you might brainstorm a list of facts and write them on a chart. Students can then pick a fact to copy onto each page.
3. Illustrate each page.

A Different Time
A Different Place

Colonial Times

A Different Time
A Different Place

The Early 1800s

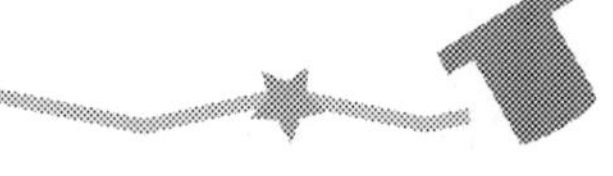

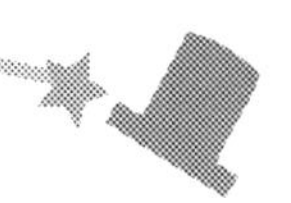

Name:

Note: Reproduce pages 51–53 to label each of the five pockets of the Presidents book.

Pocket 1

George Washington was the first President of the United States.

Pocket 2

George Washington's profile is on the front of the quarter.

Pocket 3

Abraham Lincoln was the sixteenth president of the United States.

Pocket 4

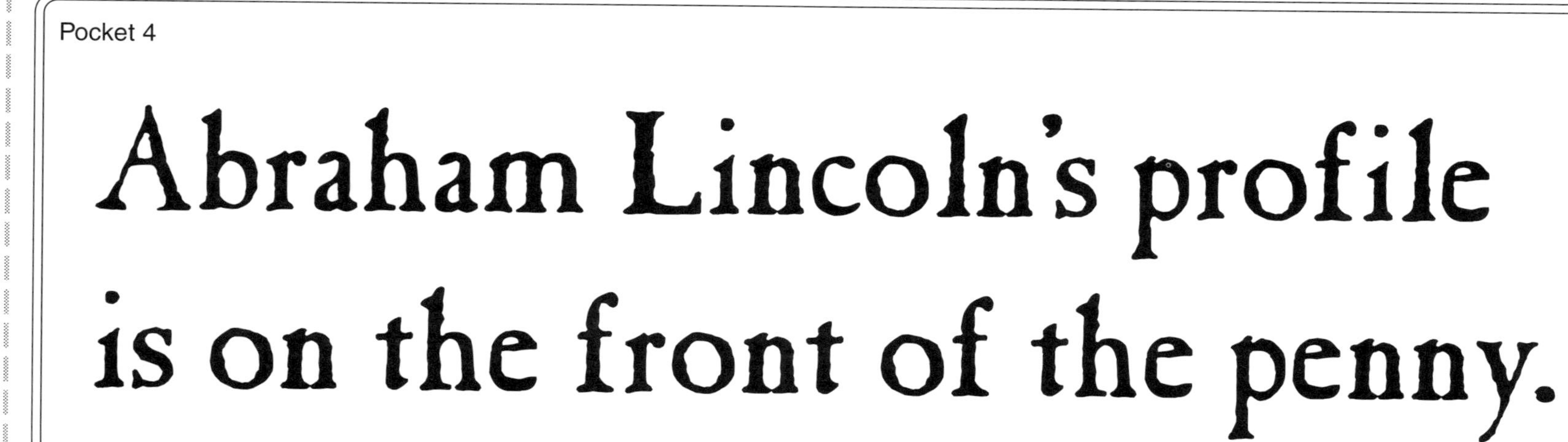

Abraham Lincoln's profile is on the front of the penny.

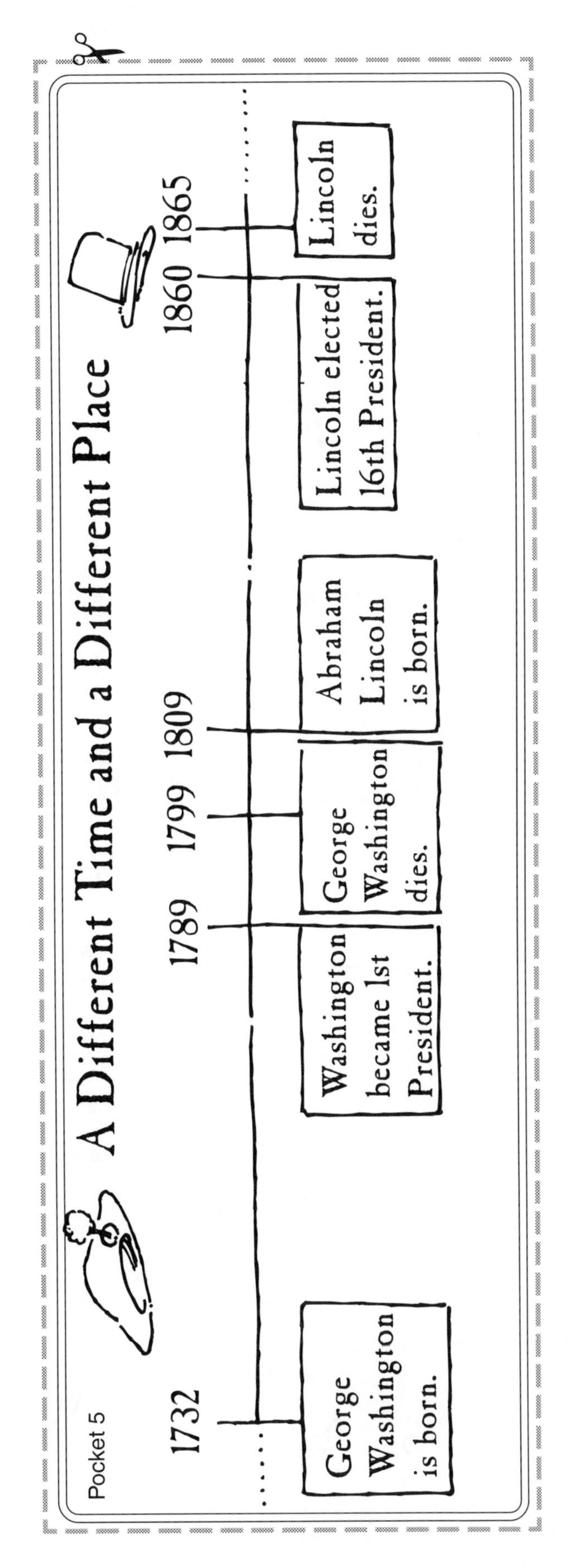
Pocket 5
A Different Time and a Different Place
1732
George Washington is born.
1789
Washington became 1st President.
1799
George Washington dies.
1809
Abraham Lincoln is born.
1860
Lincoln elected 16th President.
1865
Lincoln dies.

George Washington

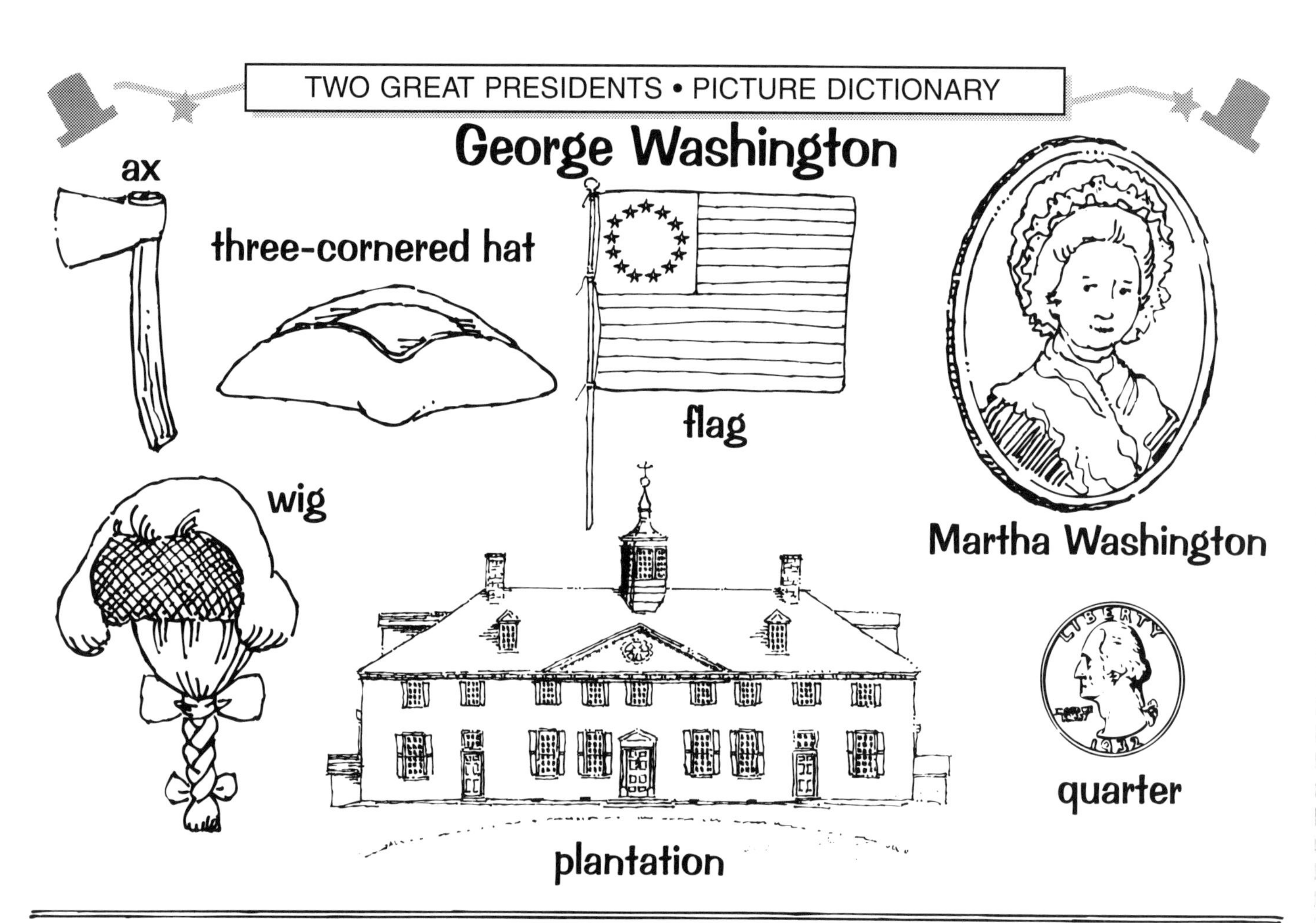

Abraham Lincoln

TWO GREAT PRESIDENTS WRITING FORM

Name:

Explore the fairy tale genre with art, written language, and critical-thinking activities in this four-pocket book. The fairy tales focused on are Cinderella, Hansel and Gretel, Sleeping Beauty, and Rumpelstiltskin.

Fairy Tale Fantasy Book Overview ____________ **pages 57 and 58**
These pages show and tell what is in each pocket.

Cover Design ______________________ **page 59**

Pocket Projects ______________ **pages 60–77**
Step-by-step directions and patterns for the activities that go in each pocket.

Pocket Labels ____________ **pages 78 and 79**

Open-Ended Forms _______ **pages 80 and 81**
Use these to aid in critical evaluation of any fairy tale.

Picture Dictionary __________________ **page 82**
Use the picture dictionary to introduce new vocabulary and as a spelling reference. Students can add new pictures, labels, and descriptive adjectives to the page as their vocabulary increases.

Writing Form ______________________ **page 83**
Use this form for story writing or as a place to record additional vocabulary words.

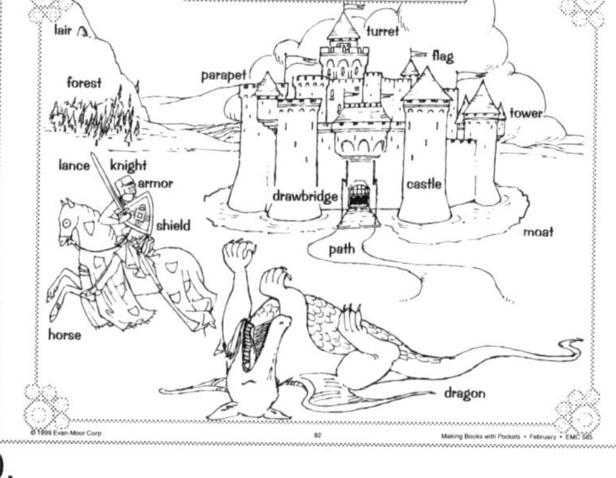

BIBLIOGRAPHY

Hansel and Gretel by James Marshall; Scholastic, 1990.
Hansel and Gretel/The Witch's Story by Sheila Black; Ariel Books, 1991.
Rumpelstiltskin by Paul Galdone; Houghton Mifflin, 1990.
Rumpelstiltskin by Paul O. Zelinsky (Illustrator); E.P. Dutton, 1986.
Sleeping Beauty by Brothers Grimm, Trina Schart Hyman (Editor); Little, Brown, 1983.
Sleeping Beauty by Lisa Ann Marsoli; Penguin Books USA, 1993.

POCKET 1

It's a Pumpkin
It's a Coach **pages 60 and 61**
After reading several versions of Cinderella, students will create a charming cut-paper coach.

My Fantastic Fantasy Vehicle **page 62**
Students write about their own fantasy vehicle.

POCKET 2

Candy House **pages 63 and 64**
As a follow-up to the tale of Hansel and Gretel, color, cut, and paste to make the witch's candy house.

Two Sides to the Story **pages 65 and 66**
After hearing the story from Hansel and Gretel's and the witch's viewpoint, students complete a Venn diagram to report the two points of view.

Giant Witch **pages 67–70**
Witches are, indeed, larger than life. This cut-and-paste witch is no exception!

POCKET 3

Prince in Shining Armor Puppet **page 71**

Sleeping Beauty Puppet **page 72**
Before putting these paper mitt puppets in the pocket, use them to reenact Sleeping Beauty's rescue.

POCKET 4

Rumpelstiltskin Flip Book **pages 73 and 74**
This flip book asks questions about the story and answers them with pictures.

Castle Writing Folder **pages 75–77**
These castle doors open to reveal students' stories written from the suggestions provided.

ALL POCKETS

Use the writing forms on pages 80 and 81 to help students think critically about the fairy tales studied. Use one or both in each pocket.

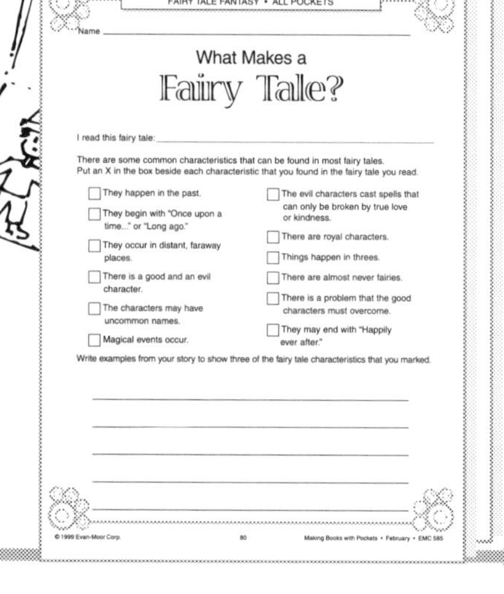
FAIRY TALE FANTASY • ALL POCKETS

Name ____________________

What Makes a
Fairy Tale?

I read this fairy tale: ____________________

There are some common characteristics that can be found in most fairy tales.
Put an X in the box beside each characteristic that you found in the fairy tale you read.

- [ ] They happen in the past.
- [ ] They begin with "Once upon a time..." or "Long ago."
- [ ] They occur in distant, faraway places.
- [ ] There is a good and an evil character.
- [ ] The characters may have uncommon names.
- [ ] Magical events occur.
- [ ] The evil characters cast spells that can only be broken by true love or kindness.
- [ ] There are royal characters.
- [ ] Things happen in threes.
- [ ] There are almost never fairies.
- [ ] There is a problem that the good characters must overcome.
- [ ] They may end with "Happily ever after."

Write examples from your story to show three of the fairy tale characteristics that you marked.

© 1999 Evan-Moor Corp. 80 Making Books with Pockets • February • EMC 585

FAIRY TALE FANTASY BOOK COVER

Note: Reproduce this cover decoration for students to color, cut out, and glue to the cover of their Fairy Tale book.

IT'S A PUMPKIN IT'S A COACH

Share a number of versions of the Cinderella story. Talk about similarities and differences among the versions. Make this pumpkin coach from the traditional European Cinderella.

Materials

- pattern on page 61, reproduced for each student
- construction paper
  coach—orange, 12" x 18" (30.5 x 45.5 cm)
  tendril—green, 1" (2.5 cm) square
  wheels—two yellow, 2" (5 cm) squares
  stem—green scraps
- scissors
- crayons
- glue

Steps to Follow

1. Color and cut out the pattern.
2. Fold the orange paper in half.
3. Glue the pattern to the orange paper.
4. Cut around the pattern, leaving a 3" fold at the top.
5. Refold the orange paper so that the pattern is inside.
6. Cut a stem from a scrap of green paper.
7. Cut the square green paper into a spiral and pull it out to make a tendril.
8. Glue the stem and tendril to the pumpkin.
9. Round the yellow squares to make wheels. Draw on the spokes.
10. Add details to the outside of the coach:
    - Windows and a door (drawn or cut)
    - Lines on the pumpkin

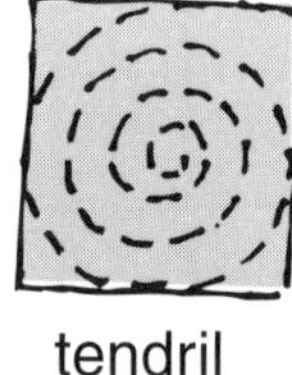

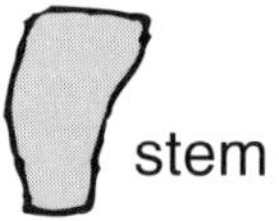

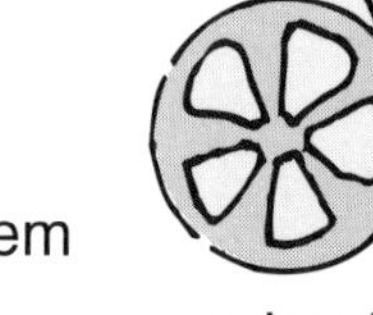

My Fantastic Fantasy Vehicle

Cinderella's Fairy Godmother whisked her off to the ball in a handsome coach magically created from a pumpkin. Tell about the fantastic fantasy vehicle you would make from something found in the garden.

I would make my fantastic fantasy vehicle from a ______________________________.

I would use these magic words to create my vehicle: ______________________________

____

Tell about what your fantastic fantasy vehicle would look like.______________________

____

____

Draw your vehicle.

Candy House

Materials

- several cotton balls
- candy house pattern on page 64, reproduced on white construction paper
- construction paper
  light blue, 9" x 12" (23 x 30.5 cm)
  pastel scraps
- crayons
- glue
- scissors

Steps to Follow

1. Brainstorm and list the kinds of candy the witch may have had covering her cottage:
   lollipops, gumdrops, candy canes, cotton candy, chocolate drops, etc.
2. Students color the candy house and add lots of candy decorations, either with crayons or cut from construction paper and glued on. Use the cotton balls to create cotton candy.
3. Cut out the candy house and glue it to the light blue paper.
4. Decorate the background by coloring with crayons and gluing on paper scraps.

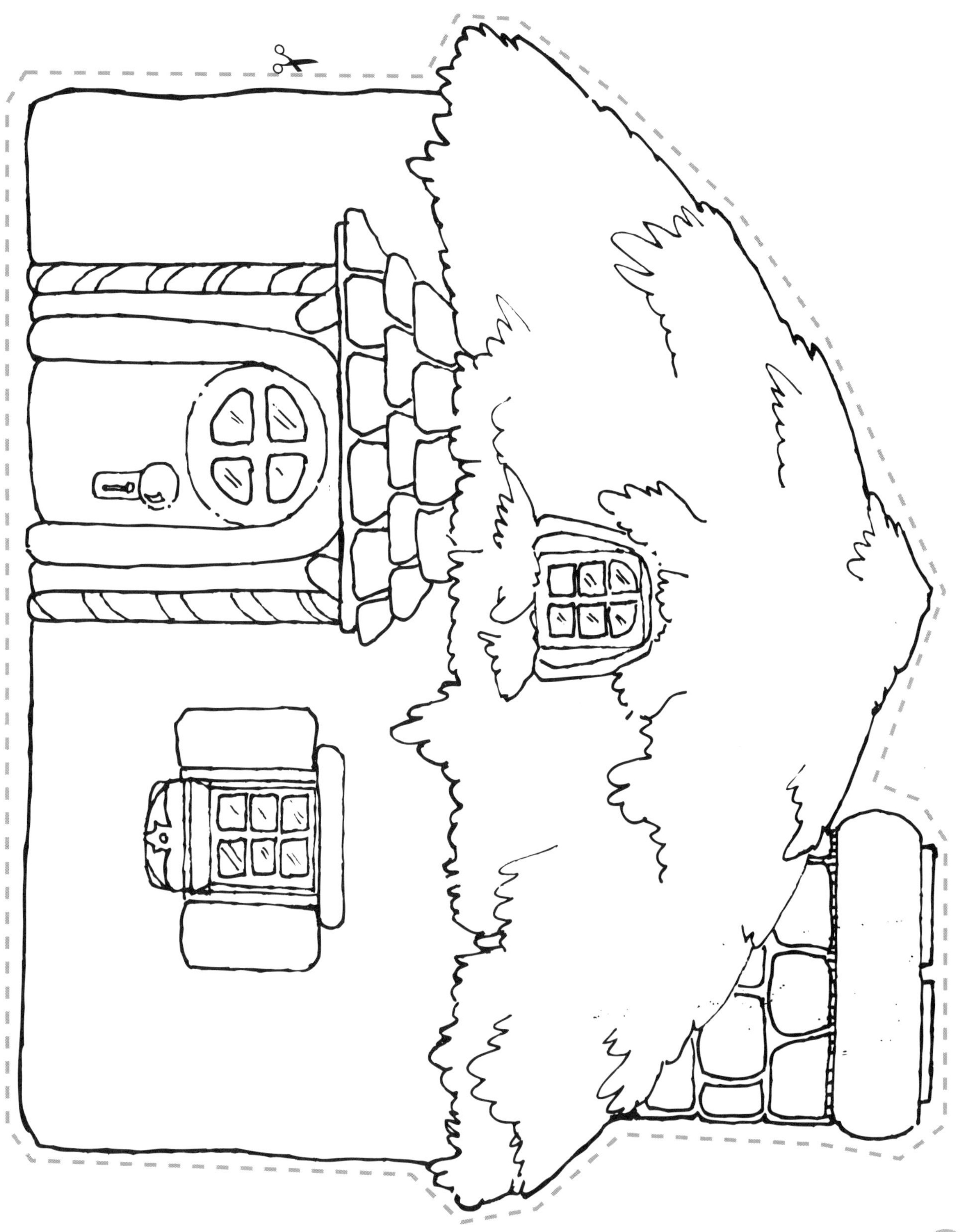

TWO SIDES TO THE STORY

Materials

- book of *Hansel and Gretel/The Witch's Story* (see bibliography, page 56)
- Venn diagram on page 66, reproduced on white construction paper
- construction paper
  witch hat brim—black, 1" x 6" (2.5 x 15 cm)
  witch hat—green, 5" (13 cm) squares
  Gretel—thin yellow strips 3"–5" (7.5–13 cm) in length

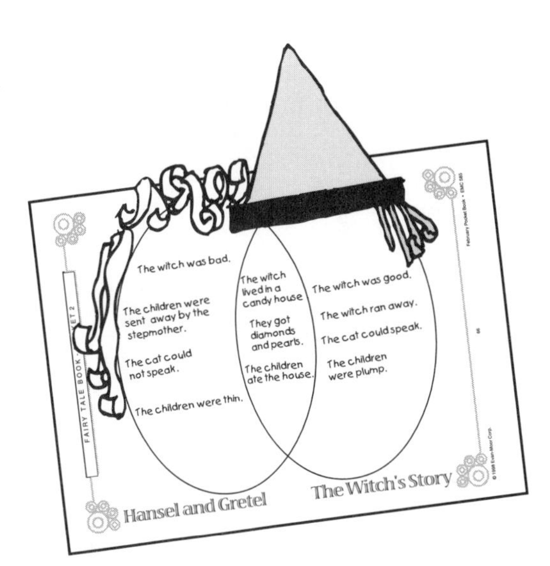

Steps to Follow

Filling in the diagram:

1. Read both sides of the story and compare the two opinions.
2. Fill in the appropriate sections of the Venn diagram with facts from the stories.

Decorating the diagram:

1. Witch's Hat
   - fold the green square in half
   - cut from the open corner to the top center to make a triangle
   - glue the triangle on top of the witch's side of the Venn diagram
   - glue the black strip on the hat
   - add some stringy green hair made from scraps
2. Gretel
   - glue yellow strips of varying lengths to the left side and top of Hansel and Gretel's side of the Venn diagram
   - curl some of the hair by rolling it around a pencil

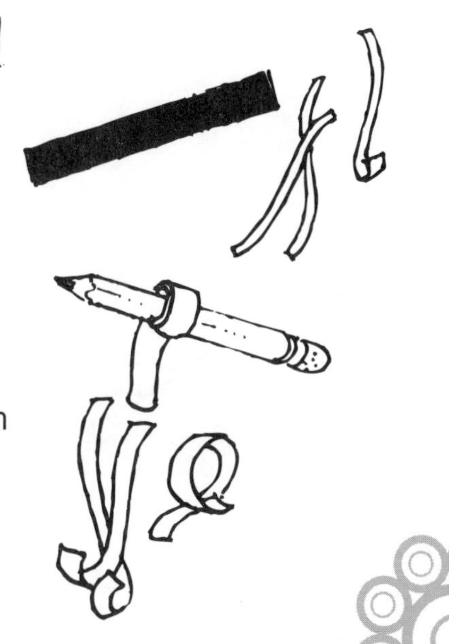

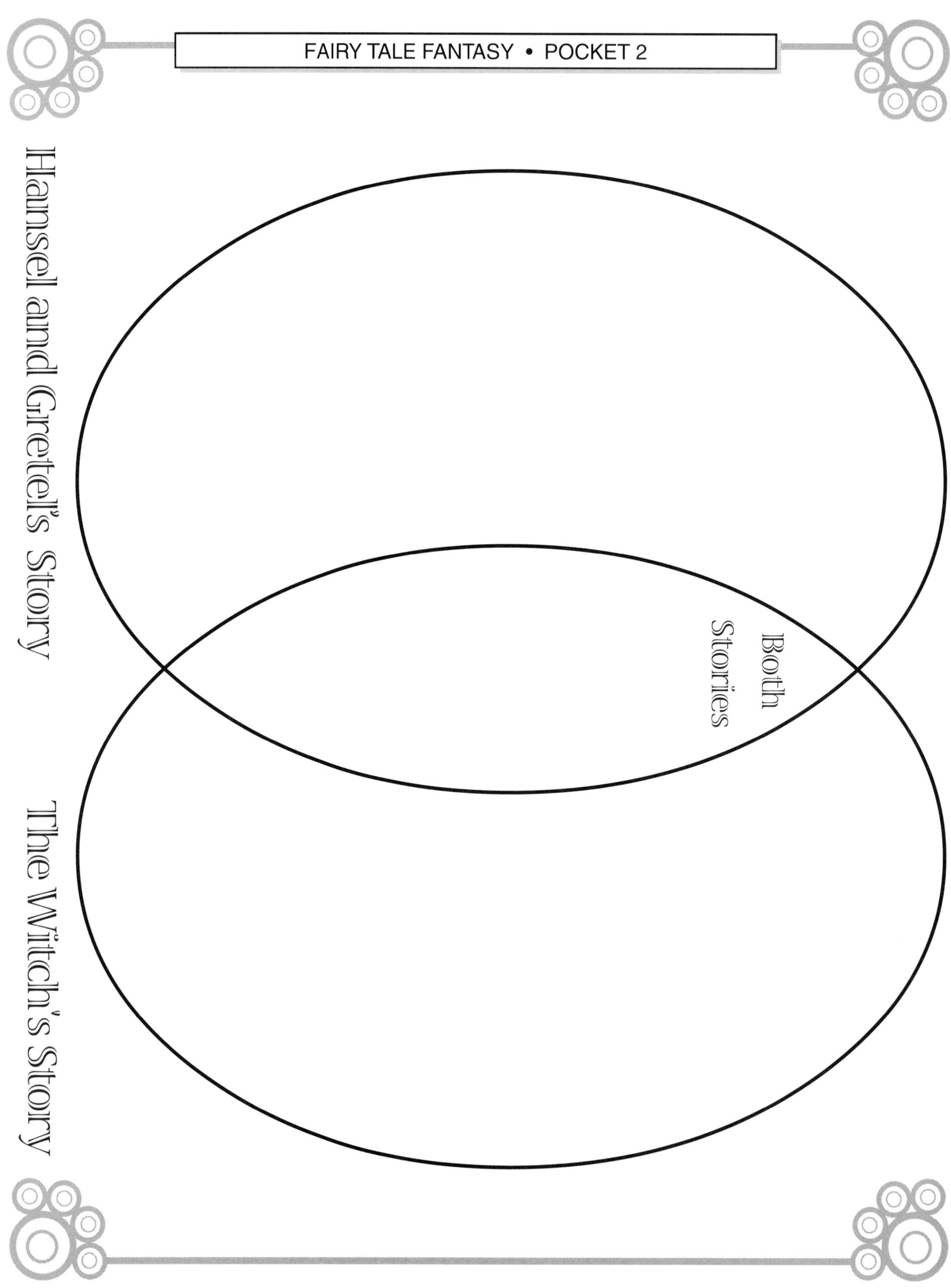
Hansel and Gretel's Story
Both Stories
The Witch's Story

Giant Witch

Materials

- patterns on pages 68–70, reproduced on manila paper
- construction paper background—colored 18" x 12" (45.5 x 30.5 cm)
- crayons
- glue
- scissors

Steps to Follow

1. Color each piece of the giant witch. Be sure to give her an unpleasant expression!
2. Glue parts together on the construction paper. Add the hair with the black crayon. The witch's hat will extend above the top of the background paper.

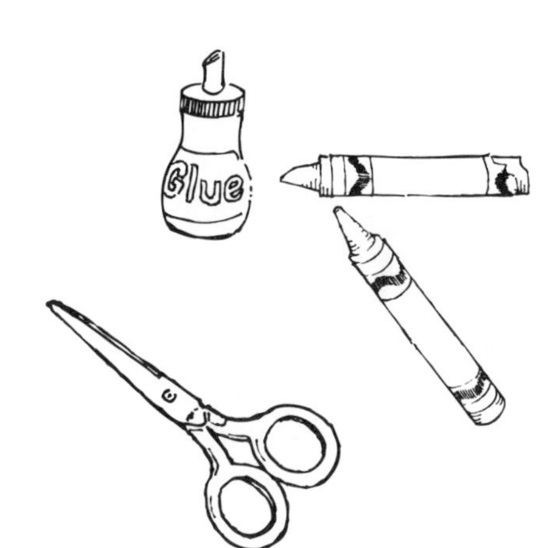

Witch's Dress Pattern

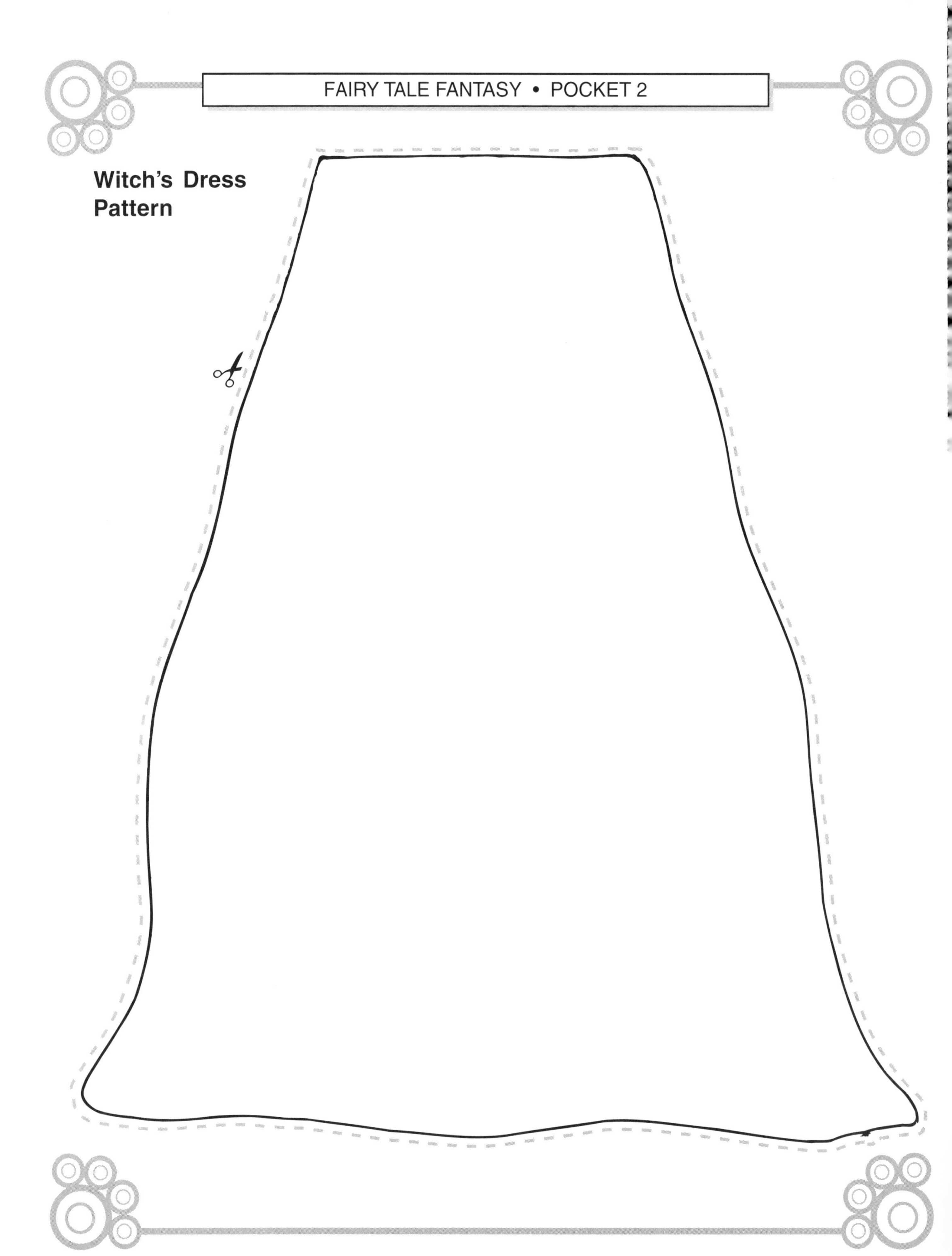

Witch's Hat and Head Patterns

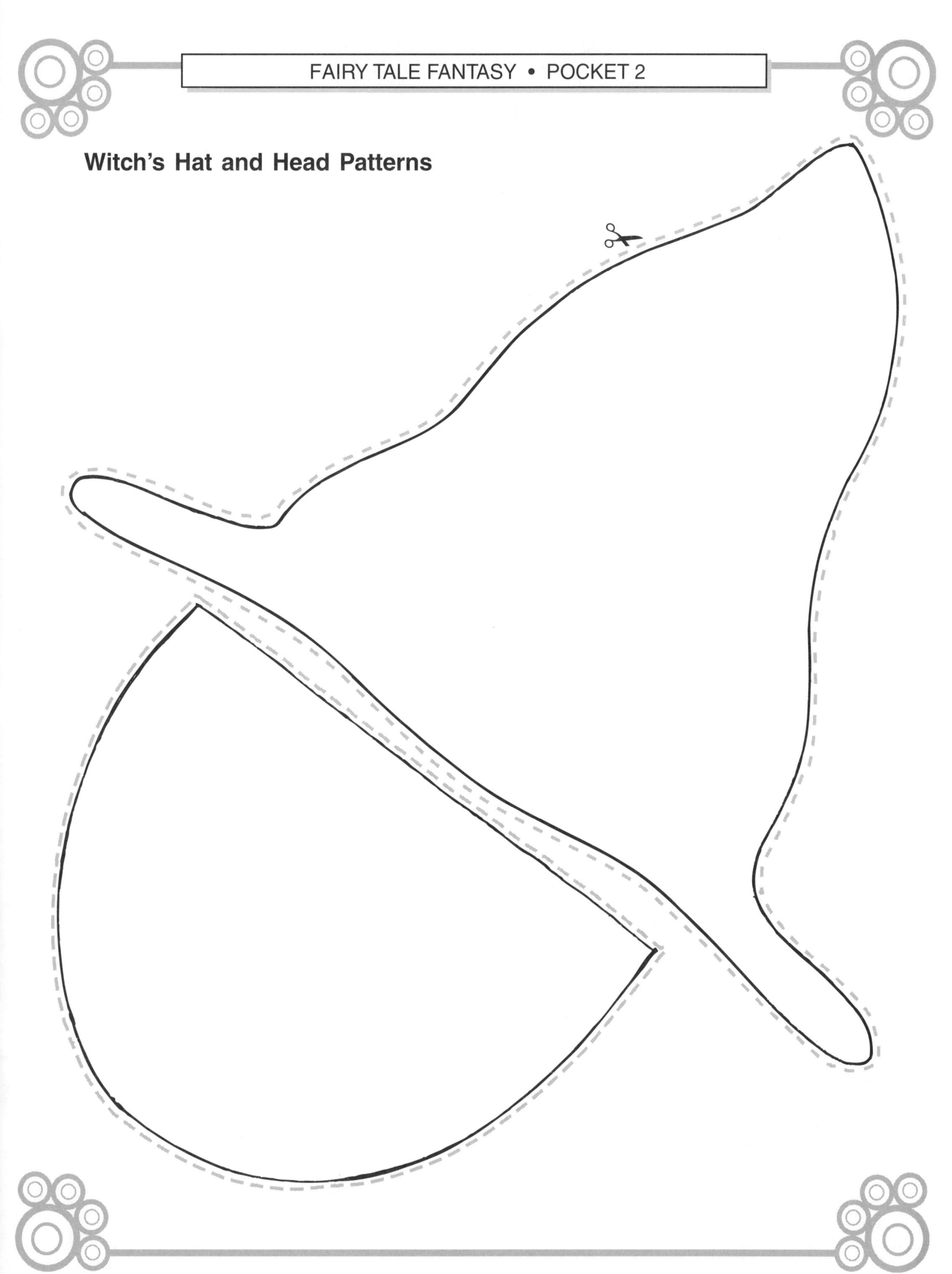

Witch's Feet and Hands Patterns

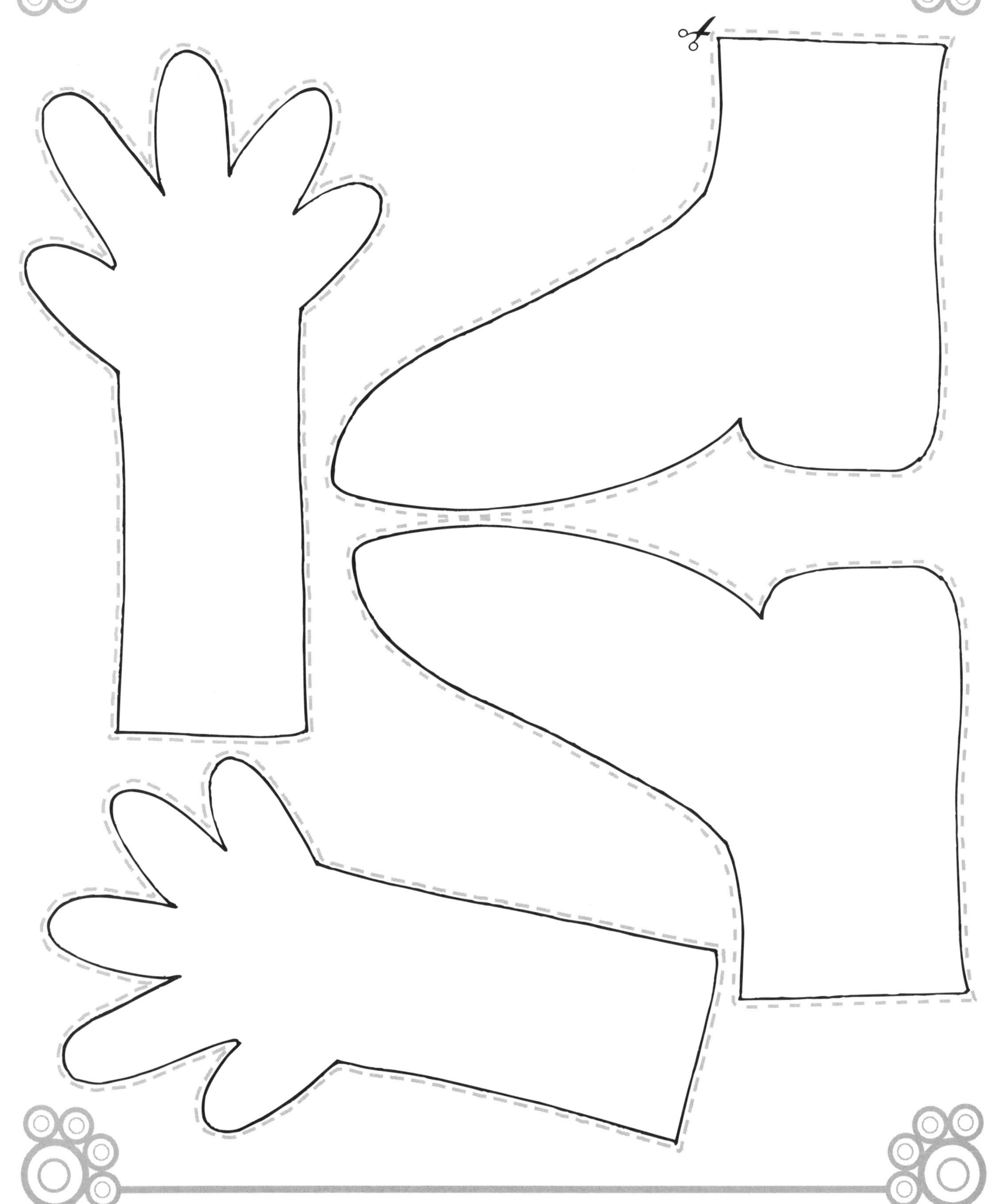

Prince in Shining Armor Puppet

Materials

- construction paper
  helmet—dark gray, 9" x 12" (23 x 30.5 cm)
  visor—dark gray, 3" x 9" (7.5 x 23 cm)
  visor slots—two black, 1" x 3" (2.5 x 7.5 cm) pieces
  visor slots—two tan, 1" x 3" (2.5 x 7.5 cm) pieces
- 5" x 6" (13 x 15 cm) colored tissue paper
- scissors
- glue
- crayons or marking pens
- hole punch

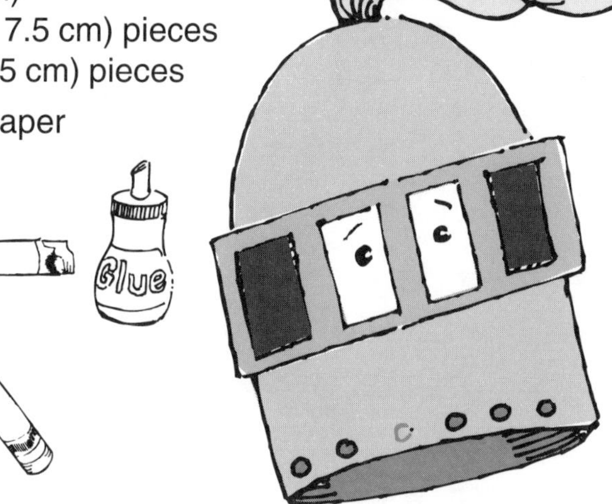

Steps to Follow

Make the basic puppet:

1. Fold the large gray paper in half the wide way.
2. Round the top corners.
3. Glue the top and open side closed.

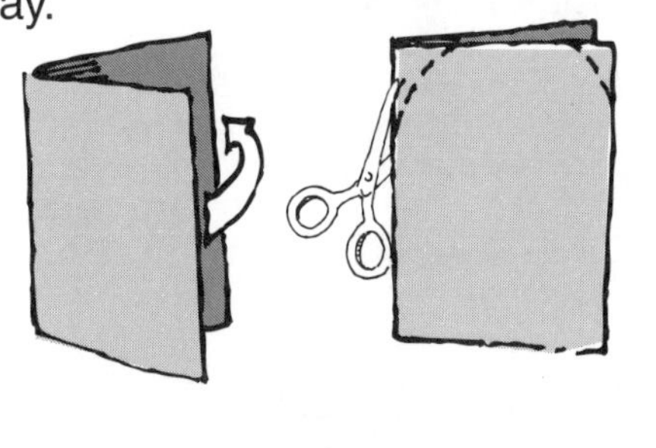

Finish the prince:

1. Glue the gray strip across the "helmet."
2. Glue the black and tan strips as shown.
3. Draw the prince looking out.
4. Make a plume from the tissue paper either by cutting a plume shape or gathering one end together. Glue the plume to the back of helmet.
5. Punch holes along the bottom of the helmet to lend interest.

Sleeping Beauty Puppet

Materials

- construction paper
  face—tan or manila, 9" x 12" (23 x 30.5 cm)
  hat—pink, 9" x 6" (23 x 15 cm)
  hair—six yellow, 1" x 9" (2.5 x 23 cm) strips
  eyes—white and blue scraps
  collar—pink, 6" x 1½" (15 x 3.5 cm)
- 1" x 12" (2.5 x 30.5 cm) tissue paper strips
- marking pens
- glue
- pencil

Steps to Follow

Make the basic puppet:

1. Fold the large tan paper in half the wide way.
2. Glue the top and open side closed.

Finish the Sleeping Beauty:

1. Curl yellow strips around a pencil to form curls. Glue to puppet front and back if desired.
2. To make hat, fold pink paper in half lengthwise and cut as shown. Glue hat over hair.
3. Use the pink strip to cut a scalloped collar.
4. Cut eyes from white and blue scraps.
5. Add other facial features with marking pens.
6. Attach strips of tissue paper to the top of the hat.

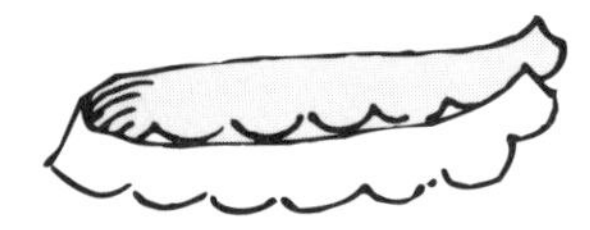

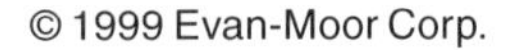

Rumpelstiltskin Flip Book

Materials

- flip book questions on page 74, reproduced for each child
- construction paper white, 12" x 18" (30.5 x 45.5 cm)
- crayons
- scissors
- glue

Steps to Follow

1. Fold construction paper in half lengthwise.
2. Fold crosswise into fourths.
3. Open paper and cut on the fold lines from one edge to the center fold as shown.
4. Fold down each flap and glue one question on each flap.
5. Under each flap draw and write the answer to each question.

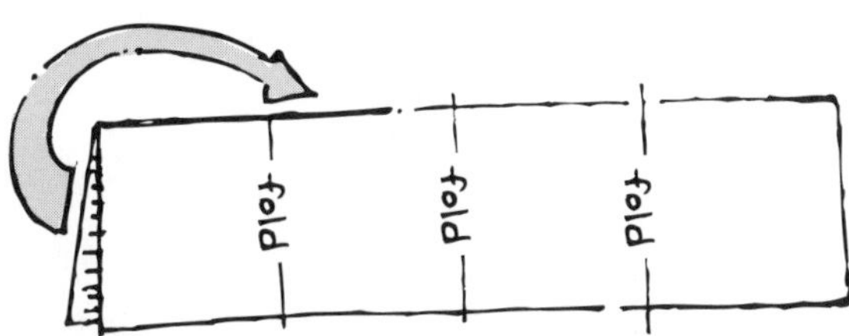

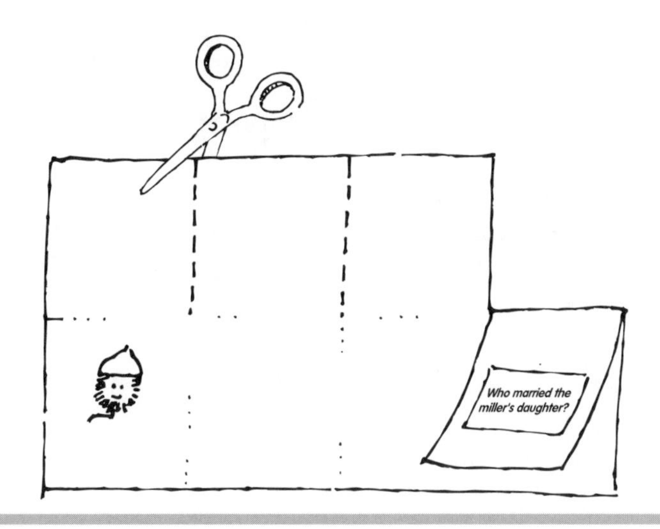

Who could spin straw into gold?

Who married the miller's daughter?

Who gave away her necklace and ring?

Who said his daughter could spin straw into gold?

Castle Writing Folder

Materials

- construction paper
  castle—gray, 12" x 18" (30.5 x 45.5 cm)
  towers—two gray, 4" x 6" (10 x 15 cm) pieces
  castle roofs—pink, 4" (10 cm) square
  tower parapets—pink, 4" x 5" (10 x 13 cm)
  doors—light brown, 4" (10 cm) square
  windows—black and yellow scraps
  flags—colorful scraps
- scissors
- glue
- writing form on page 77

Steps to Follow

Fold the basic building:

1. Fold the large gray paper in half the long way.
2. Open up and fold in half the other way.
3. Fold each end to the center.
4. Fold down corners, opening outside flaps.

(directions continued on page 76)

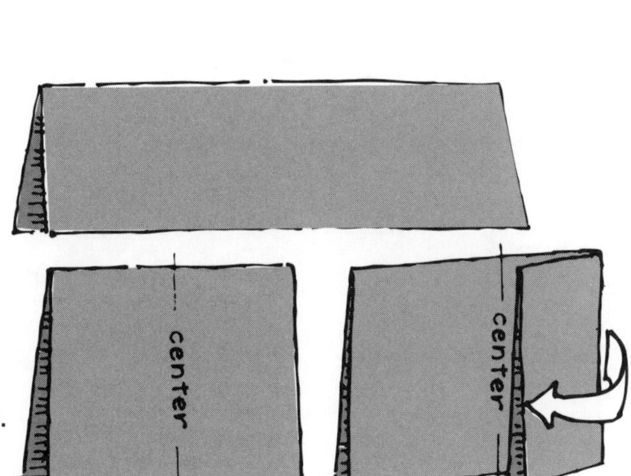

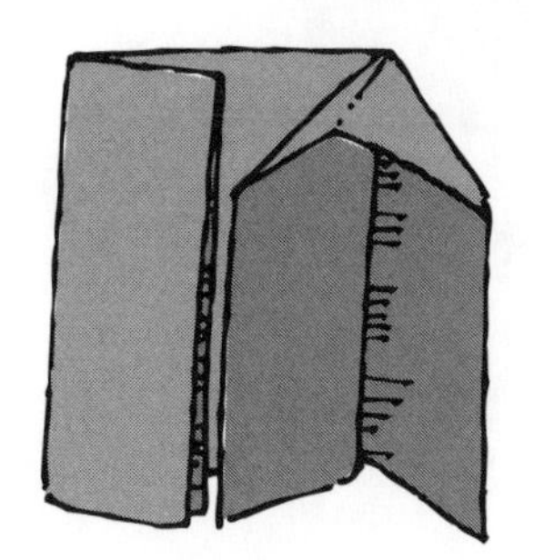

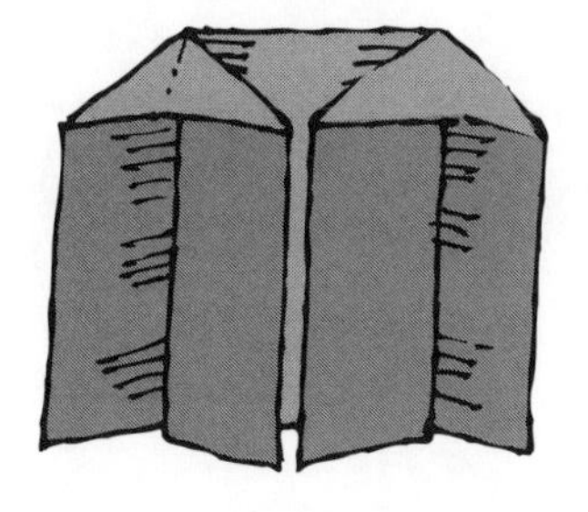

Making the castle:

1. Glue the gray rectangles to the back to create towers that extend about 2" (5 cm) above the peaks of the roof.
2. Cut the pink square in half diagonally. Glue these triangles onto the roof peaks.
3. Fold the pink rectangle in half the long way and cut.
4. Make ½" (1.25 cm) cuts along one long side about every ½" (1.25 cm). Cut out every other section to form parapets.
5. Glue the parapets to the tops of the towers.
6. To make the castle doors, round the top corners of the light brown paper. Fold in half and cut into two pieces. Glue on either side of the center opening.
7. Use scrap paper to make windows and flags.

Writing Suggestions

1. Write a fairy tale about a royal family.
2. Retell a fairy tale that involves a castle. Change something to make your tale different. For example:

   Cinderella—What if the clock in the prince's castle stopped before midnight?
   Rapunzel—What if the prince was afraid of heights?

3. Choose a fairy tale. Describe and draw the main characters.

Note: Reproduce this page and page 79 to label each of the four pockets of the Fairy Tale book.

Cinderella

Pocket 1

Hansel and Gretel

Pocket 2

Sleeping Beauty

Pocket 3

Rumpelstiltskin

Pocket 4

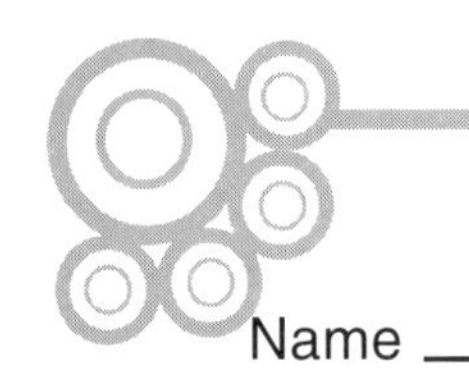

Name ______________________________

What Makes a Fairy Tale?

I read this fairy tale: ______________________________

There are some common characteristics that can be found in most fairy tales.
Put an X in the box beside each characteristic that you found in the fairy tale you read.

- ☐ They happen in the past.
- ☐ They begin with "Once upon a time..." or "Long ago."
- ☐ They occur in distant, faraway places.
- ☐ There is a good and an evil character.
- ☐ The characters may have uncommon names.
- ☐ Magical events occur.
- ☐ The evil characters cast spells that can only be broken by true love or kindness.
- ☐ There are royal characters.
- ☐ Things happen in threes.
- ☐ There are almost never fairies.
- ☐ There is a problem that the good characters must overcome.
- ☐ They may end with "Happily ever after."

Write examples from your story to show three of the fairy tale characteristics that you marked.

____

____

____

____

____

Name ______________________________

____

Title

Villain

I am a bad character in this story because...

____

Hero/Heroine

I am a good character in this story because...

____

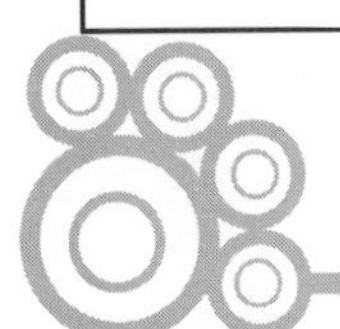

FAIRY TALE FANTASY PICTURE DICTIONARY

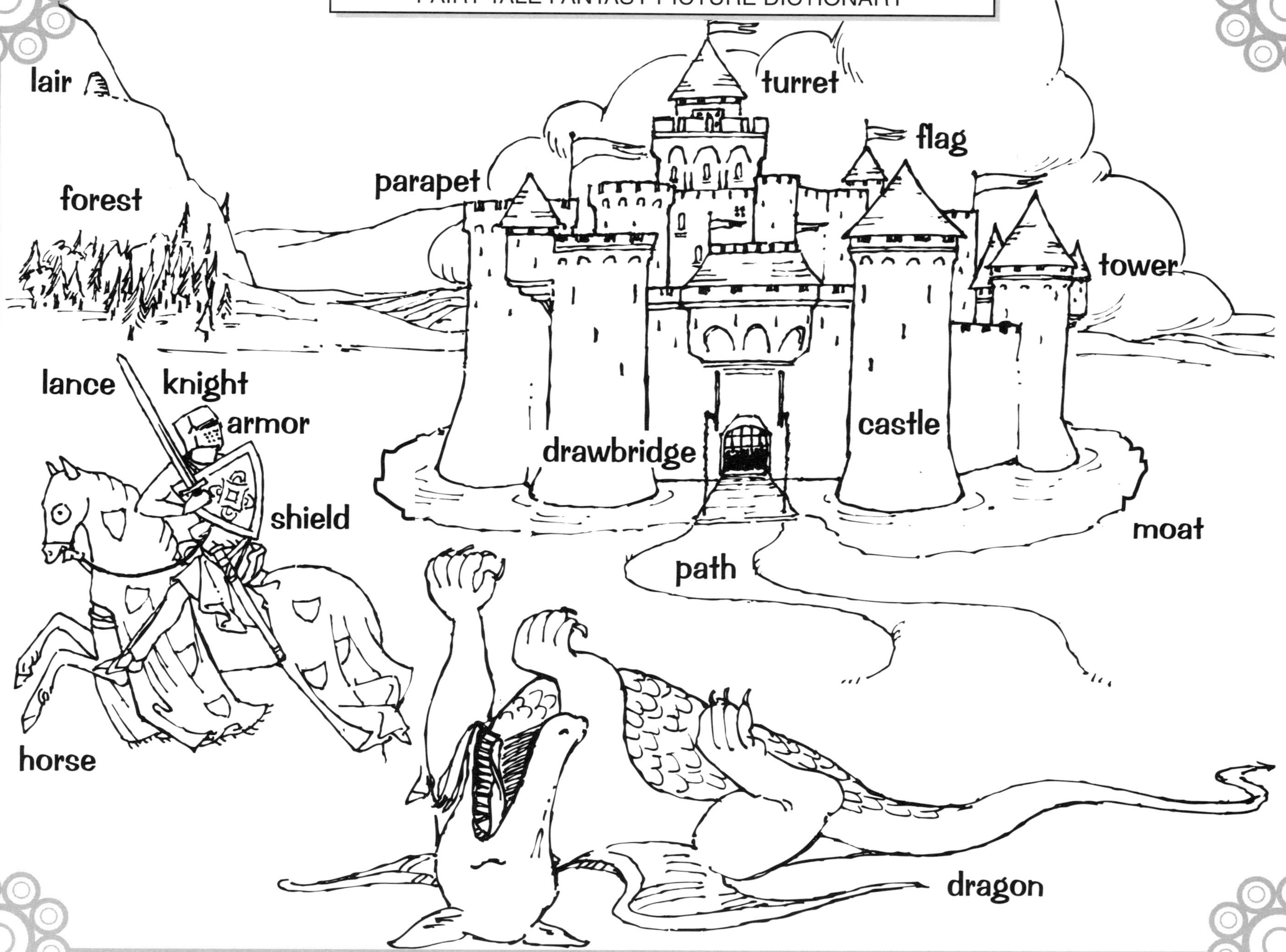

lair
forest
lance
knight
armor
shield
horse
parapet
turret
flag
tower
drawbridge
castle
moat
path
dragon

FAIRY TALE FANTASY WRITING FORM

Name: ____

Two Great Presidents—pages 85–92

Using this interactive bulletin board, students sort facts about George Washington and Abraham Lincoln and place them in a pocket under the correct president's picture.

Display books on Washington and Lincoln near the bulletin board. Students research additional facts, write them on index cards, and add these fact cards to the container.

Abraham Lincoln once worked splitting fence rails.

George Washington chose the place where the White House was built.

There is no proof that George Washington chopped down a cherry tree.

February Coordinate Pairs—pages 93–96

Pictures of February objects are placed on a grid. Students name the coordinate pair of each picture's location. The February pictures can be moved regularly, creating lots of practice throughout the month.

Vary the practice by having students pick task cards that show a picture and the coordinates. Students place the picture at the correct point on the grid. For example:

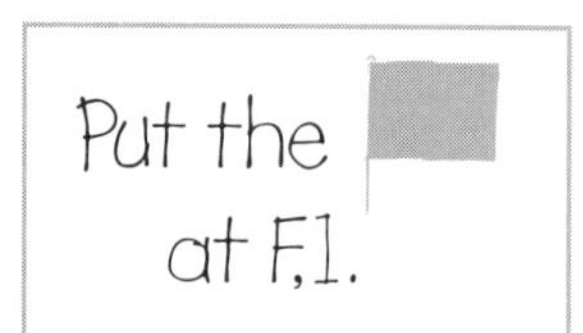

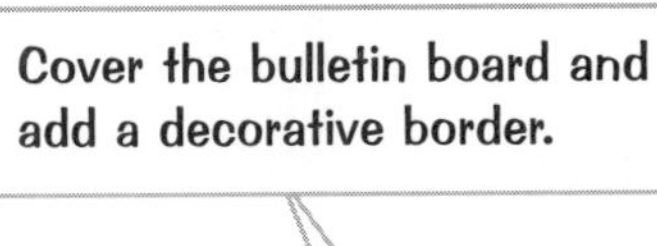

Cover the bulletin board and add a decorative border.

Cut the banner from butcher paper.
Add portraits from pages 86 and 87, mounted on red or blue construction paper.
Two Great Presidents
George Washington
Abraham Lincoln
He was a lawyer.
Mount fact cards on pages 90–92 on construction paper and place in a container.
Create pockets by stapling plastic strips to the board.
Reproduce the task cards on pages 88 and 89 and mount on red or blue construction paper.

Materials

- blue butcher paper
- red butcher paper
- patriotic trim
- presidents' portraits on pages 86 and 87
- task cards on pages 88 and 89
- fact cards on pages 90–92
- blank 5" x 8" (13 x 20 cm) cards
- four 9" x 12" (23 x 30.5 cm) red and blue construction paper
- twelve 4½" x 6" (11.5 x 15 cm) red and blue construction paper
- four 3" x 20" (7.5 x 51 cm) clear plastic (acetate or laminating film) strips
- stapler
- container for fact cards
- books about Washington and Lincoln

George Washington

Abraham Lincoln

Read the books about George Washington and Abraham Lincoln. Look at the facts about these two presidents on the cards in the container. Place each card in the pocket under the president it describes.

Use the books to find your own fact about Washington or Lincoln. Write it on a card and place it in the pocket under the president it describes.

He believed owning slaves was wrong.

He lived in the White House with his wife Mary and his three sons.

He made a famous speech at a battlefield in Gettysburg, Pennsylvania.

The Civil War was fought during his presidency.

He was born in Kentucky
and grew up in Springfield,
Illinois.

He was a lawyer.

He was a Virginia farmer.
The name of his home was
Mount Vernon.

He owned slaves.

He was the Commander in Chief of the American army during the Revolutionary War.

Many people wanted him to become the king of the United States. But he said "No." Later he became the first President of the United States.

He was born on February 22, 1732.

His picture is on every one-dollar bill.

February
Coordinate Pairs

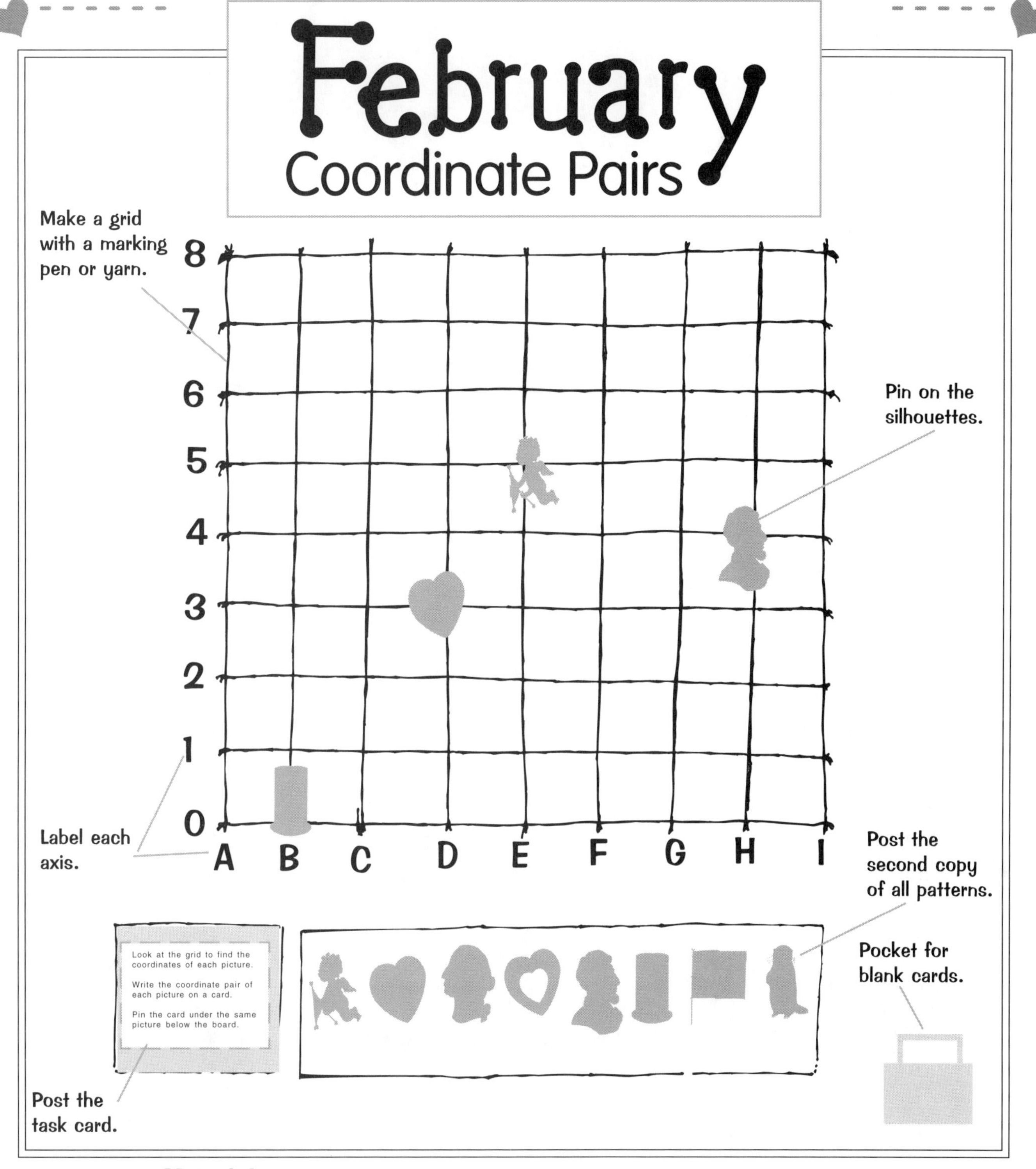
Make a grid with a marking pen or yarn.
8
7
6
5
4
3
2
1
0
A B C D E F G H I
Pin on the silhouettes.
Label each axis.
Post the second copy of all patterns.
Look at the grid to find the coordinates of each picture.
Write the coordinate pair of each picture on a card.
Pin the card under the same picture below the board.
Pocket for blank cards.
Post the task card.

Materials

- task card on page 94, mounted on construction paper
- 3" x 2" (7.5 x 5 cm) cards
- two copies of patterns on pages 95 and 96, cut from colored paper
- two colors of yarn (optional)
- T pins
- marking pen

Look at the grid to find the coordinates of each picture.

Write the coordinate pair of each picture on a card.

Pin the card under the same picture below the board.

Math Grid Pictures

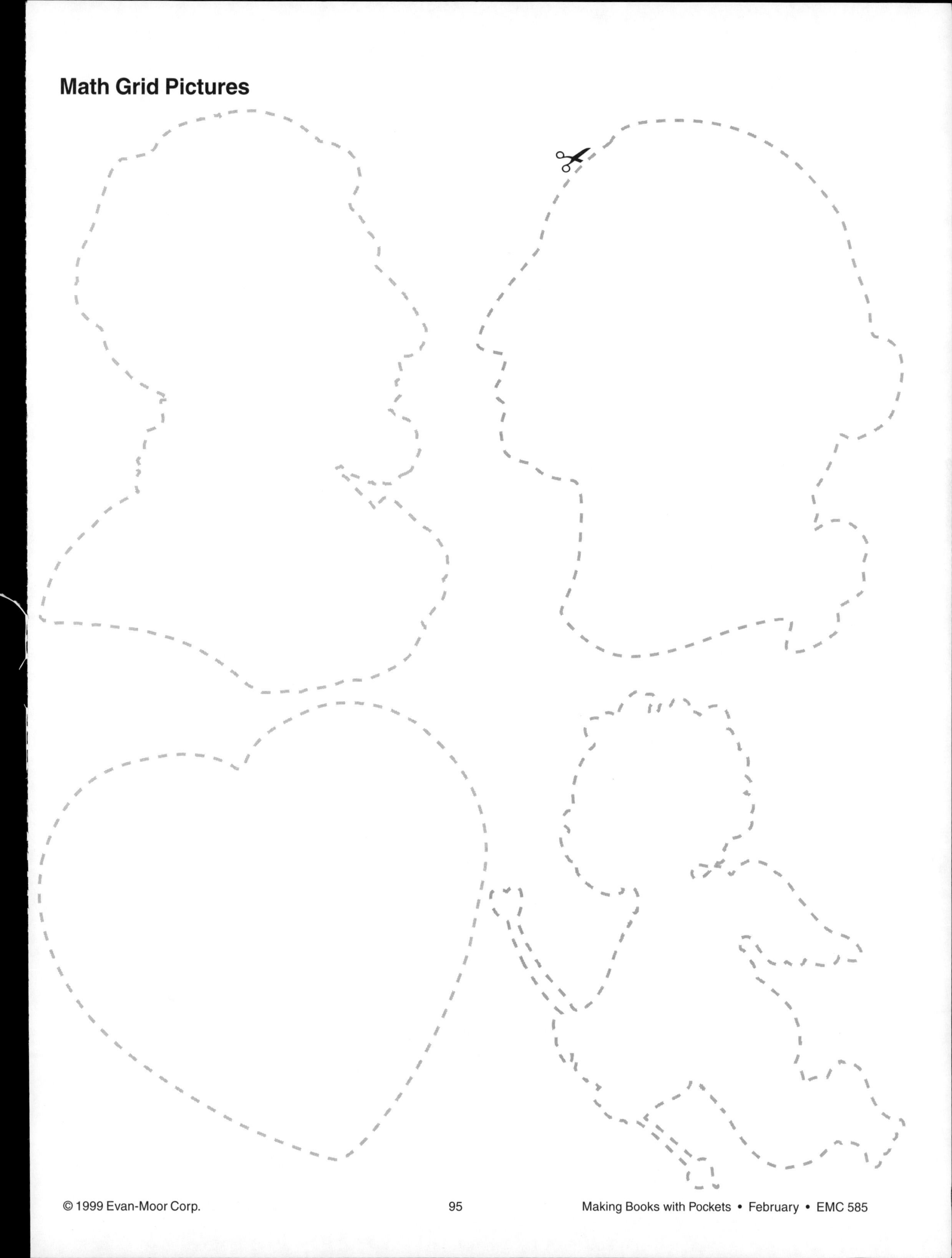

Math Grid Pictures

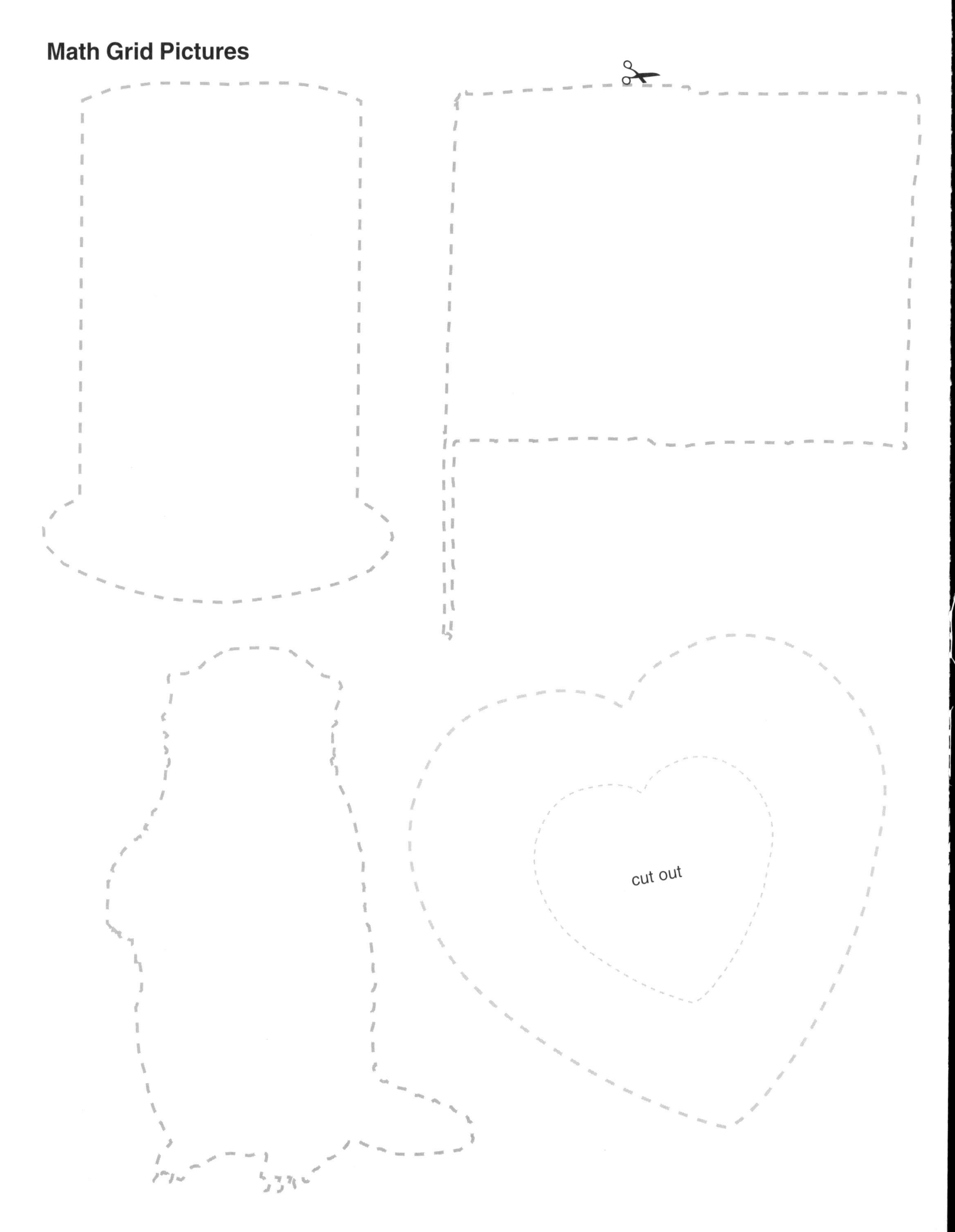